Team-Smart
SQ

Synergy Pals Help You
Discover Your Synergy Quotient…
What it Means to be Smarter Together.

Ardys U. Reverman, Ph.D.

Think   **Look**   **Talk**   **Feel**

This Book Belongs To

Jon Wolf

*Synergy puts create greater
results working together —
warmly Gody*

Color Me Sense-sational!

ii

Here's what some synergy leaders have to say about
Team-Smart SQ

"The Synergy Pals rekindle the rich spirit that those who differ from us give to our lives, to explore the world from four points of view and compare that world to our own with those who matter most in work and play." *MEGA SERIES*

Jack Canfield and Mark Victor Hansen, co-authors, *Chicken Soup for the Soul*

"To understand our lives as lifelong opportunities of learning is to claim the spiritual road into wholeness."

The Right Reverend Rustin Kimsey, Episcopal Bishop of Eastern Oregon

"We are all different. Dr. Reverman has captured those differences in this work and made it easy and natural for child and adult to get back into the understanding mode, so that everyone in the family can be comfortable and accepted."

Lendon H. Smith, M.D. , author, *The Children's Doctor*

"What drives people... to be right, to be liked, to seek attention, to have control, to protect family and everyone you know. Easily, affordably, redefine what it means to be smart. One people living on one planet."

Tony Alessandra, Ph.D., author, *The Platinum Rule*

"I am pleased to be able to add my support to the work you are doing in the latest brain research, new and exciting body of knowledge to the field in education."

Anthony R. Palermini, former superintendent DDSD, Oregon

"If we help children learn in their own way today, they will be able to give their best talents tomorrow working in synergy teams."

Debbie Autzen, Realtor, and Scott Thomason, CEO, Thomason Auto Group

"Understanding the different ways people process information is an important skill we use all our lives."

Susan Hammer, attorney at law-mediator, and Lee Kelly, sculptor

"Diversity means families in everyday relationships, sharing fun and learning. For real success learn to understand differences where everybody counts."

Nickyanne Laman, Founding Diamond Sales Director, Discovery Toys

"The cornerstone of effective management and the number-one edge over competition is that people must like you and trust you. In a competitive world the edges are extremely important."

Bill Reilly, president, William Reilly Engineering

"The inner game of business is whole-brain communication. It is a valuable tool to develop successful marketing skills for your personal and business creativity."

Helen M. Rockey, CEO

"An easy and smart beginner's guide to the basics of understanding how temperament works together to create God's Cosmic Joke. Reconciliation propels us."

Nancy Kelley, Nancy's Concepts Unlimited---www. singleangels.com

"Both science and common sense show us our view of human intelligence is far too narrow. We ignore a crucial range of abilities that matter in terms of how we succeed in life. Being emotionally fit gives you the strength to express your uniqueness. "

Douglas Houser, attorney, Bullivant, Houser, Bailey, Pendergrass & Hoffman

"Synergy Pals Profile is an easy personality assessment tool to enlighten and entertain while exploring human needs for relationship."

C.G. Cale, Investment Manager

"Parents and professionals are most effective by making us feel self confident by valuing teamwork. We shine at feeling really good about beng smarter together."

Carlita and Ron Evezich, Evezich Enterprises

"When pulling a garment together we start the creative process with color, followed by silhouette. Then we begin the engineering of technique and measurement, which completes the style. This is a creative, whole-brain process."

John H. Herman, CEO Duffel Sportswear

"Analyzing scripts and changing directors' minds to improve all parts of production uses the whole brain in a way so that every sense counts."

Gordon Kee, Motion Picture Producer

"Listening to your customer-centered needs ensures a win-win benefit for all."

William Barendrick, Jr., former President, Oregon Assoc. of Realtors

"Redefining "smart" for the love of it, gets everybody into the act, for we are the first generation to be aware of ourselves as a WHOLE ."

Patricia Fripp, past president, National Association of Speakers

"Lifelong, we must take on new tasks in order to exercise the thinking and feeling sense of all things that keep our brains healthy."

Cameron Truesdell, CEO Long Term Health Care

"Conscious choices and unconscious forces bring an idea like Feng Shui whose time has come; uncover your strengths for interior work you love to do."

Dana Barton Cress, Interiors

"Working together means winning teams, when we understand how our different strengths create a goodness of fit."

Chris Cusick, president, Cusick's Talent Agency

"I think the strength of the book is in the examples of how the SQ styles interact in the real world. Different situations can threaten each of the personality types into different expressions of self need and discord."

Barbara Swanson, M.L.S., founder-president, Catalyst Bookseller

"A profound appreciation of the whole team can lead to championships when w skillfully play our own part well. Teaching is more than the sum of the parts."

Peter J. Ness, award winning coach

Team-Smart
SQ

Synergy Pals Help You

Discover Your Synergy Quotient...

What it Means To Be Smarter Together

By Ardys U.Reverman, Ph.D.

Illustrated by
Charlotte Lewis

1993-#1-*All About You in the Creative Circle*
1999-#2-Newly Revised and Expanded Edition
Library of Congress Cataloging in Publication Data
Reverman, Ardys U.

Team-Smart SQ
Synergy Pals Help You Discover Your Synergy Quotient...
What It Means To Be Smarter Together

Summary: A read-aloud book that helps people develop control of creative temperament strengths to understand partnership in a new synergistic way.
p. 223 cm.
1. Self-respect. 2. Self-perception. 3. Success—Psychological aspects.
4. Personality development. 5. Temperament strengths.
6. Parental acceptance. 7. Cognition I Title. 8. Collaboration

BF697.5.S54.R	1999
158.1 20	98-060225
	CIP

ISBN 0-9625385-1-5

Dedicated lovingly to my Mama and Papa,
now in the light of God's heart.
By living kinship, we reach beyond self,
link up differences, reweaving
the ongoing circle of
the friendly universe.

Agreement
of
Collaboration

Synergy Pals Int'l has dedicated this material to provide information in regard to the subject matter covered. It is sold with the understanding that the publisher and authors are not liable for the misconception or misuse of information provided. Every effort has been made to make this information as complete and accurate as possible. The purpose of this information is to educate.

The author and Synergy Pals Int'l shall have neither liability nor responsibility to any person or entity with respect to any loss, damage, or injury caused or alleged to be caused directly or indirectly by the information contained herein.

They shall not be liable for the completeness or accuracy of the contents of the books and products in this series.

Foreword

It is difficult to put emotions and feelings into words, not just for children, but for mature, wise adults. There is no doubt that we could learn better skills to communicate with our children and each other. While animals smell each other, humans guess another's emotions by what is shown on the face: anger, love, boredom, anxiety, fear, pain, etc. We can do the Haim Ginott strategy of "I see you are angry. Can you tell me about it?" But who remembers what to ask when one is tired or distracted?

We also know that people are different; some are hyper, some are calm and collected, some learn by doing, some learn by hearing or feeling or reading. We are all different. Dr. Reverman has captured those differences in this work and made it easy and natural for child and adult to get back into the communication and understanding mode so that everyone in the family can be comfortable and accepted. Once that has happened, children develop good self-images. This is the chief purpose for childhood — to achieve a positive self-concept so that when that child matures, he or she will be a contributing, fulfilled adult. Parents have given their children a good self-image, which is the chief job for childhood.

Lendon H. Smith, M.D.

(Lendon Smith is the most recognized "children's doctor" in the nation and author of many books including *Hyper Kids, Improving Your Child's Behavior Chemistry, How to Raise a Healthy Child — Medical and Nutritional Advice from America's Best-Loved Pediatrician*)

"There are only two or three human stories, and they go on repeating themselves as fiercely as if they had never happened before."

Willa Cather

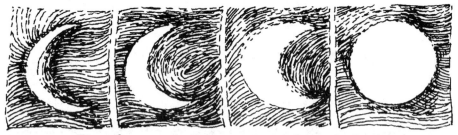

Preface: A Message for Adults
Learning Together with the Synergy Pals

The Synergy Pals takes you (parent, grandparent, family member, educator — any caring adult) on an interactive journey of self-discovery with your child. This book is meant to be read aloud and shared together, as partners. Through fun and personal explorations, you and your child will discover your own personality styles and how you can best relate to each other. After you learn how easy it is to recognize the various personalities (the Synergy Pals), you will be able to unite the tensions of opposite styles into a positive, compatible synergy — a way to work and play smarter together. Knowledge is an active verb of love and shared power. Reconciliation propels us.

As you go along, encourage your child to participate by coloring the pictures in the book. Colors have special meanings here, representing four personality characters, the Synergy Pals. Each Pal has a special style of learning, living and feeling: There's the step-by-step thinking process of Think-about Owl, the hands-on practice of Feel-about Koala, the Talk-about Chimps message (don't kill a messenger of new ideas) and the back-from-the-future visions of Look-about Lion. Together, (like you and your child) they form a co-creative team. Our brain makes sense of our senses. Experience is food for brain development. We learn to think about wishes and wants in a new way.

A Child's Personality Development

Though you and your child may be of different personality (or temperament) types, it is the fit, not the type, that determines the course of the child's development. We all need to learn what we are good at and how we fit in. Then we can successfully develop our own natural gifts for self-fulfillment and make the most of our relationships with others. Understanding our own personality style begins with understanding how we all learn and grow. Brain/mind research tells us that we learn more and retain more of what we learn when we are alert, relaxed, and feeling safe. When we approach change naturally and with pleasure, we have far better results in terms of both our intrapersonal intelligence (knowing who we are) and our interpersonal intelligence (learning from and helping each other).

Our thoughts generate desires, motives, and values; these are felt and expressed as needs, which lead us to act. If our own personality remains unknown or unacknowledged, and our needs fail to be met, we may live as an enigma inside and out, constantly flip-flopping between miserable isolation and clinging dependency. This instability can lock us into a lifetime of inappropriate behavior. Though a true personality style may be masked for years, ultimately it will manifest itself.

If we, consciously or unconsciously, become too polarized by our own personality type, we lose the freedom to choose to act differently. Then it becomes easy for us to spend a lifetime seeking and conflicting with our polar opposites. Consider how people are so often attracted to their opposite personality type—the orderly with the spontaneous, the agreeable with the controlling, the reflective with the expressive, the exacting with the generalizing. The tensions of opposites co-create and co-evolve us. Our natural desire to interact with other, including the wish to help our children, is frequently misunderstood and rejected when our personality type does not match that of the other. This may result in arguments, withdrawal, and alienation. Technically, we may be saying all the right words, but we still need to understand how to satisfy the needs of others' hearts by learning to speak each other's emotional language. This language comes from one's own particular personality and determines how each of us interprets and interacts with the world around us. We create a good learning fit.

Synergy explained puts another spin on the ball of perception that much of who we are is determined by boy and girl brain differences: the on/off switch of multi-tasking and talking for girls, and the focus skills of the hunt for boys. Brain research is robust. Hormones, and socializing influences can channel this boy and girl biology into life's creative forces. Smarter together boys and girls have their own separate way of doing things given the right drive, skill and nurturing. The more we understand how we and others think, learn, and interrelate, the more we can contribute to the intellectual and emotional development of our children and to our healthy, joyful relationships with them.

The Shared Power of Synergy

As Alfred Korzybski reminds us, "The map (our experience) is not the territory (the world)." Each of us perceives a different and equally real reality. We see things as we are, not as they are. Ideally, we use our interactions with the world to explore our reality, to question it, to stretch its boundaries, thereby moving the whole circle of learning back to our true selves.

Our mind either locks us into a limited "flat" worldview or hurdles us over the fear of the unknown so we can stretch beyond our own viewpoint. Then we can incorporate new visions and possibilities by embracing how we all learn individually and collectively, as a silent significant whole.

Einstein's theory of relativity has helped us to see the benefits of a totally connected universe. We can interact powerfully within this natural framework by forming chains of awareness. Understanding, then links us with other people so we all have access to each other's talents. This co-creative view of synergy may sound complicated, but it's easy to see how it works when you and your child start playing along with the Synergy Pals.

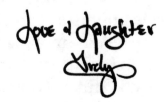

"*A* *human being is a part of the whole, called by us 'Universe,' a part limited in time and space. He experiences himself, his thoughts and feelings as something separated from the rest — a kind of optical illusion of his consciousness. This delusion is a kind of prison for us, restricting us to our personal desire and to affection for a few persons nearest us. Our task must be to free ourselves from this prison by widening our circle of compassion to embrace all living creatures and the whole of nature in its beauty. Nobody is able to achieve this completely, but the striving for such achievement is itself a part of the liberation and foundation for inner security."*

Albert Einstein

Thinkabout Owl, Lookabout Lion,
Talkabout Chimp, and Feelabout Koala
learn how to stay healthy and have fun
through all of the work and the play,
one and all, every day.
For each is a part of the Whole.

Thinkabout Owl,Lookabout Lion,
Talkabout Chimp, and Feelabout Koala
all name their troubles and tell themselves,
Now I'll learn from the rest
and still be my best for
I am a part of the Whole.

Table Of Contents

"Something we were withholding
made us weak
Until we found it was ourselves."
Robert Frost

"We dance 'round the ring and
suppose, but the secret sits in
the middle and knows."
Robert Frost

SENSE-sational
Synergy Pals

If you could look inside your thoughts through a magic window, what do you suppose you'd see?

You'd see the different parts of your personality, the values, beliefs, and feelings which affect your thinking and behavior. This helps you discover what you really want and how satisfied you'll feel when you see you're a whole person with a mind and hidden talents of your own.

The magic window is like a prism with four colors showing the thinking lights inside.

When you look through the magic window, you'll see animals with colors green, blue, yellow, and red, just like your own four points of view —Think, Look, Talk, and Feel.

These animals show us different ways of looking at the world, through colors, seasons, and our inner moods.

We see things as we are, not as they are. Your thoughts color your own inner map and your point of view.

The animals are just another way of looking at the different parts inside of **YOU**, and others, too.

You'll see a little bit of yourself in each one of the four animals. It's the match that counts. The whole is joining us in a new way.

As you learn more about them, your heart may tell you that one of the four is more like **YOU** than the others and more special to you. Which one is most like **YOU?** Ask your heart and then imagine . . . what were you born to do best?

The magic window reveals the natural talents inside of you.

The
Sense·Sational

Imagine your four senses
seeing things from
four points of view as a . . .

Think-about Owl,

Look-about Lion,

Talk-about Chimp,

Feel-about Koala.

Which one is most like **YOU** right now? At different times, you'll see that each Synergy Pal is a think, look, talk, and feel sense inside you. You also learn to stretch from the Synergy Pal least like you. The match or mismatch of these senses is what counts. We all learn to choose better, take responsibility for ourselves and get much better results by following through with our agreements.

Talkabout Chimp
Inspires
Ideas

Talkabout Chimp

When I'm a Talkabout Chimp

If I were a Chimp, a Talkabout Chimp,
ideas would whirl through my mind.
They'd dance 'til I'm crazy and
twirl 'til I'm dizzy,
until I can barely unwind.

I'm good at pretending,
expressing, inventing,
I'm artist and actor at play.
I'm often creative
and so innovative,
I do everything in a new way.

I like to be out
with nature about.
There's so much to
hear 'neath the sky.
A talk with my friend
is the very best way
to catch the ideas that fly by.

I love to talk to friends about ideas,
and I have so very many questions.

I crave understanding,
I can be demanding,
my wishes not easily met.
With your indecision,
mocking or meanness,
I'll frown and I'll fidget and fret.

If you reject me it hurts.
Ignoring's the worst
kind of treatment
I'll ever endure.
Then I put things off,
withdraw, become moody,
feeling very unsure.

*I love it when I can
do something new and different.*

I love to question the rules
and the reasons
and do what seems right to me.
I need your affection and
true understanding
to feel that I really am free.

So, give me a hand;
please listen and lend
your thoughts to the projects I've planned.
For I need to know
that I can be friends
with someone who does understand.

*When I have fun with friends
putting on a show, I feel great!*

13

Talkabout Chimp

When I'm a Talkabout kind of person, I need to feel understood, to share my ideas and be creative.

I like to . . . (*check the boxes most like you*)

- ☐   hear people explain how to do something.
- ☐   choose what I want to learn.
- ☐   shout with joy.
- ☐   find different ways to do an assignment.
- ☐   hear people talking in soft, nice voices all around me.
- ☐   talk to myself while I do a problem or task.

- [ ] talk about what scares me or makes me angry or happy.
- [ ] talk in a loud or quiet voice, whichever sounds best to me.
- [ ] hear about legends and myths and what other people believe.
- [ ] talk while everyone listens to my ideas.
- [ ] share my ideas first, and see how others react.
- [ ] play games that use my ideas and imagination.
- [ ] do lots of different things at the same time.
- [ ] be in plays, where I can express myself.

Talkabout You

Who listens to and understands me?

What questions are on my mind today?

If I were going to do a show, what kind of show would it be?

Am I someone who likes to share ideas, listen and talk,
have hunches in bunches and be the one who loves
to have fun?

Through my Talkabout window, I share inspired ideas
and dreams. I know how to understand others
and be understood.

Am I a Talkabout Chimp who likes to listen and talk
about ideas and have understanding?

"I know but one freedom, and that is the freedom of the mind."
Antoine de Saint Exupery

Thinkabout Owl Practices Carefully

Thinkabout Owl

When I'm a Thinkabout Owl

If I were an Owl, a Thinkabout Owl,
you'd find me alone in my room
enjoying the quiet, enjoying my thoughts,
so don't interrupt me too soon.

Oh, I love to ponder
the meaning and wonder,
the workings of this and of that . . .
the order of numbers
and patterns and rhythms
of systems and logic and maps.

I like my room neat
and it's really a treat
for me to arrange it my way,
so don't wait around
for a finishing sound,
I just might be busy all day.

*I'd be amazed to see on paper all the figurings and
feelings going through my mind in just one day.*

I need things in order,
a predictable future
with everything tidy and straight.
If things get too messy
or plans get too iffy,
how can I expect to create?

When I am aware of
confusion and scared,
I freeze,
and don't know what to do.
Then I may get
stubborn, unfriendly, aloof,
and even
stop talking to you.

It's okay for me to like details and
want things in order.

Now please understand
that I do need a friend, and my
feelings don't know what to say.
You'll just have to know
that I like you although
I seem to be running away.

I really like facts, with
step-by-step lessons.
I'll do the best work that I can.
So, tell me exactly what you expect,
and I'll produce the ideas you plan.

Just give me some time
for being alone,
to put my surroundings to mend.
Then I'll be ready
for more conversations
and riddles and games with my friend.

*When I feel safe, it's easy for me to work and have fun
with others, even very different types of people.*

Thinkabout Owl

**When I'm a Thinkabout kind of person, I need
to know everything is in order, safe, and correct!**

I like to . . . *(check the boxes most like you)*

- [ ] take my time before I act on an idea.
- [ ] use skills I already have.
- [ ] explain ideas step by step.
- [ ] earn my own spending money.
- [ ] read about how things are discovered and the reasons why they are special.
- [ ] control my own things and have a special place where I make the rules.

- [ ] know exactly what to do.

- [ ] have all my things lined up in order.

- [ ] not have to tell others how I really feel if I'm upset.

- [ ] be on time and have my friends be on time to meet me.

- [ ] be loyal to my friends and take good care of my pets.

Thinkabout You

Whom do I feel safe with and like to do things with?

What's going through my mind today?

What sort of things do I most like to keep in order?

think·about owl

Am I someone who likes to sit in my room where I feel safe as I quietly think and work by myself? Do I like to figure things out carefully and put everything in order?

Through my Thinkabout window, I know how to gather details, making plans to keep order and safety.

Am I a Thinkabout Owl who likes to be safe at home and have things in order and time to think?

"**B**irds build their nests in circles, for theirs is the same religion as ours."

Black Elk

Lookabout
Lion Leads
Tomorrow

Lookabout
Lion

When I'm a Lookabout Lion

If I were a Lion, a Lookabout Lion,
the world would be mine to explore.
I'd be a leader or clever inventor
of what's never been tried before.

My plans are so huge,
so tall and so wide
they go far into reaches of space.
I wish to move forward
and upward and onward
and follow my vision someplace.

I'm a person of action.
I see the attraction
of having control of my fate.
I like to take charge
of projects so large,
and, with others, accomplish the great.

I know I can build wonderful things — houses, boats, and giant rockets to explore outer space.

So don't get in my way
or make me delay
the task I've set for myself.
For I must be free
to do wondrous deeds —
not tied up or put on the shelf.

And if I feel caged,
I'll roar and I'll rage,
I'll yell, I'll demand, and I'll snap.
I'll quickly take action
in any direction
that might get me out of a trap.

I'm brave and always ready to explore.
I can see in my mind a plan that will get things done.

I always need freedom
and room to move on.
I hate things that get in my way.
You may feel amazed,
confronted, and dazed
or hurt by the things that I say.

Please understand,
that's the way that I am,
it's the way I try to break free.
Don't cower or cringe
if your feelings get singed,
just stand up and tell it to me.

*I feel good when everyone cooperates to do one of my
projects, and I feel proud when I can take charge
to make sure the job is done well.*

Lookabout Lion

When I'm a Lookabout kind of person, I need to feel free, have choices, and get results!

I like to. . . (*check the boxes most like you*)

- ☐ imagine what life will be like in the future.

- ☐ choose by myself the direction I want to go.

- ☐ search for solutions to problems.

- ☐ work on something that takes a long time.

- ☐ have a quiet place where I can think.

- ☐ watch somebody work while they explain to me what they're doing.

- [ ] choose clothes in my favorite colors that make me look good.

- [ ] look at pictures in books and read stories that explain the how and why of things.

- [ ] draw diagrams to explain my ideas.

- [ ] see by people's smiling faces that they like me.

- [ ] have lots of pencils, colored markers, and big sheets of clean paper for my use.

- [ ] talk or listen only when I want to.

- [ ] have the colors and things around me look nice and neat.

- [ ] go to museums or other interesting places and explore them for as long as I want.

Lookabout You

What would I invent and what places would I explore?

What plans or projects do I have now?

What projects have I done well with others?

Am I someone who likes to have choices and wants to make quick decisions? Am I able to work out a plan in my mind and get results on any project I choose?

Through my Lookabout window, I see a world to explore and know I have the freedom to take charge.

Am I a Lookabout Lion who likes to get results, have lots of choices, and be a free spirit?

"*A fellow can't think or feel accurately unless he knows something.*"
Mark Twain

Feelabout
Koala
Tugs
Hearts

Feelabout Koala

When I'm a Feelabout Koala

If I were a Koala, a Feelabout Koala,
you'd find me surrounded by friends.
For I love to chatter
with people who matter.
I hope that the fun never ends.

I help all my friends to get along well
and help them be part of a team.
With everyone working
and playing together,
I'm flexible, smiling, and serene.

My favorite place to sit is the sofa,
surrounded by pillows and rugs.
I'd like to feed everyone
cookies and cocoa,
cheerfully giving them hugs.

I love to do nice things for my friends,
especially give gifts to them.

45

But tell me you're angry,
or bluster and yell,
and you'll find me shrinking away.
Don't make me feel silly
and shove me around
or I'll struggle to get my own way.

"Poor me!"
can be snappy, whiny, and prickly
when I am feeling left out.
To get me involved,
praise my help with some friends.
Believe me, you don't have to shout.

*I love to sit in a cozy chair and daydream
about happy people helping one another.*

47

Just give me a part
to play in each game,
with everyone getting along.
A crowd where people
are working together
will help me to feel I belong.

I love to have harmony,
smiling and sweet,
I sing when I'm part of the plan.
And I hunger for compliments
coming from you;
they make me feel precious and grand.

*I love parties and the gentle laughter of
my friends while we all eat together.*

49

Feelabout Koala

**When I'm a Feelabout kind of person, I need to feel
in harmony with everything around me,
that my feelings matter and I belong.**

I like to . . . (*check the boxes most like you*)

☐   learn by doing and making things with my hands.

☐   hug and be hugged by people I like.

☐   have noisy fun.

☐   know everybody is a friend to me.

☐   dance all around to music.

- [ ] ride my bike fast, feeling the wind on my face and the movement of my body.
- [ ] wear clothes that are neat, but it's okay for me to get them dirty or rumpled.
- [ ] listen only as long as I want to.
- [ ] sit in any chair I want, whenever I want.
- [ ] feel it's okay to let everyone know how I feel.
- [ ] work on something right away and think about what I'm doing as I go along.
- [ ] not have to pay attention to the clock.

Feelabout You

Whom have I helped who appreciated what I did?

Who are the people I like to be with?

What sorts of things do I like to make with my hands?

feel·about koala

Am I someone who loves to touch and make things?
And when I know that everyone around me is friendly,
do I like to share my feelings and talk?

Through my Feelabout window, I feel how to create
harmony and help friends get along with one another.

Am I a Feelabout Koala who likes to touch things, feel
in balance and be with my friends?

"*It is the theory that decides what we can observe.*"
Albert Einstein

The Synergy Pal Most Like You

Now you know whether you are a Thinkabout, Lookabout, Talkabout, or Feelabout kind of person most of the time. Try a stretch with the Synergy Pal least like you. See yourself with your mind's eye, take responsibility for yourself and get better results by following through with your agreements. Remember it's the match that counts.

Each person has his or her own natural talents, which is a certain way of belonging in the world. We are really at our best when we bring *all* the parts together, from the inside out.

Your Natural Talents

And now for an easy quiz to learn about your natural "thinking" talents . It's not a test, though. The purpose of this quiz is to make it easy to know your natural talents in thinking. All you have to know is something about yourself. This quiz will reveal the way you most like to be, your urges, and the actions you like to take in the world. What you're willing to do, that is important to you.

Your personality has an overall pattern that tells you what you're willing to do, and how you can make sense of the behavior of others. Understanding, order, freedom and harmony turn the creative circle of values connecting us all within the Friendly Universe, which continues on and on.

Each value plays a role in the whole. Take some time to think about the following questions and answer them carefully. They'll tell you what you want to know. Every answer is right.

Thinkabout   Lookabout   Talkabout   Feelabout

Answer the questions according to the very strongest feelings you have about each one. This is the easiest and most natural way for you to understand your own deeply-rooted values — understanding, order, freedom, and harmony. Thinking is enjoyable when we are aware of our values and feelings. Understanding something about why we turn out the way we do.

How you like to act when you think, see, hear, and feel is important. We arrange our feelings in our minds. We have a longing to lead a joyful life. We are born to choose what is most true for us, so our quiz answers are always correct.

Because other people have different talents and think, see, hear, and feel things differently, they will answer the questions differently.

After you have finished the quiz, you may find it interesting and fun to talk about your different answers with your friends.

**For each question,
consider how you feel.**

Give a four (4) to the answer **MOST** like you.
Give a three (3) to the answer **Next-to-most** like you.
Give a two (2) to the answer **Next-to-least** like you.
Give a one (1) to the answer **LEAST** like you.
Don't use the same numbers twice.
Here's an example of how to answer the questions:

I like...

a. to have things in Order my way. [2] The answer next-to-least like me.

b. the Freedom to get things done. [1] The answer least like me.

c. the Harmony of getting along [4] The answer most like me.
with my best friends.

d. Understanding my inspired [3] The answer next-most like me.
dreams in a new way.

---

1. I feel happiest with myself when I am . . .

a. helping my friends get along together and
being thanked for my help .... ☐

b. putting my belongings in order
so I can find things when I need them .... ☐

c. sharing my new ideas to inspire
others to seek their own new ideas .... ☐

d. visualizing a plan and explaining
how to get it done quickly and correctly .... ☐

2. I work best when I can . . .

a. work with others and be shown how
to do things by someone who knows how .... ☐

b. think and work quietly on my own,
following directions step by step .... ☐

c. watch what someone else does well, plan
how I will do it, and get it done .... ☐

d. tell others my new ideas, inspiring them
to risk doing things in a new way .... ☐

**Add up the numbers going down in each
column of boxes. Put the total in the
matching box at the bottom of the page.**

☐ ☐ ☐ ☐

3. When I'm with others talking and listening, I . . .

a. first watch and listen, then freely share my big
plan about when, what, why and how to do it ......

b. first enthusiastically tell of my great new ideas,
then I want to hear if others understood me ....

c. warmly ask about others' feelings and
share my feelings in a friendly, helpful way ....

d. just politely listen until I'm asked
what I think; then I quietly answer ....

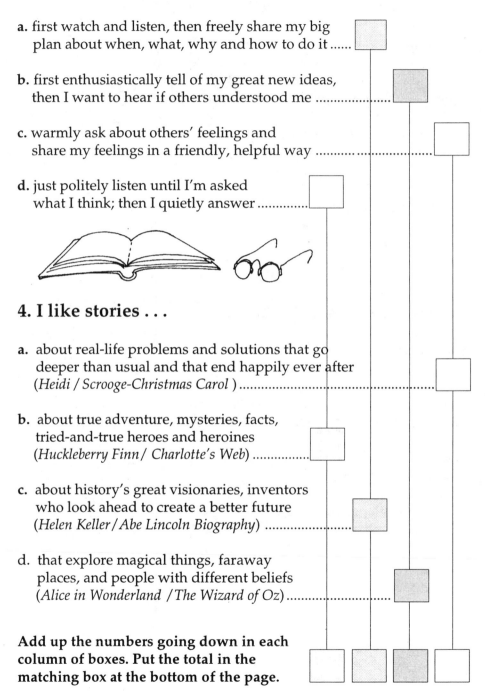

4. I like stories . . .

a. about real-life problems and solutions that go
deeper than usual and that end happily ever after
(*Heidi / Scrooge-Christmas Carol*) ....

b. about true adventure, mysteries, facts,
tried-and-true heroes and heroines
(*Huckleberry Finn / Charlotte's Web*) ....

c. about history's great visionaries, inventors
who look ahead to create a better future
(*Helen Keller / Abe Lincoln Biography*) ....

d. that explore magical things, faraway
places, and people with different beliefs
(*Alice in Wonderland / The Wizard of Oz*)..............

**Add up the numbers going down in each
column of boxes. Put the total in the
matching box at the bottom of the page.**

5. I solve my problems or make decisions best when . . .

a. I feel secure enough working in a
group to ask other people to help me...

b. I know the facts that tell me exactly
what to do to get the right answer...............

c. I plan things my own way by comparing
good and bad ideas to get quick results.................

d. I brainstorm with others, trust hunches, and
discover a new way to put ideas together........................

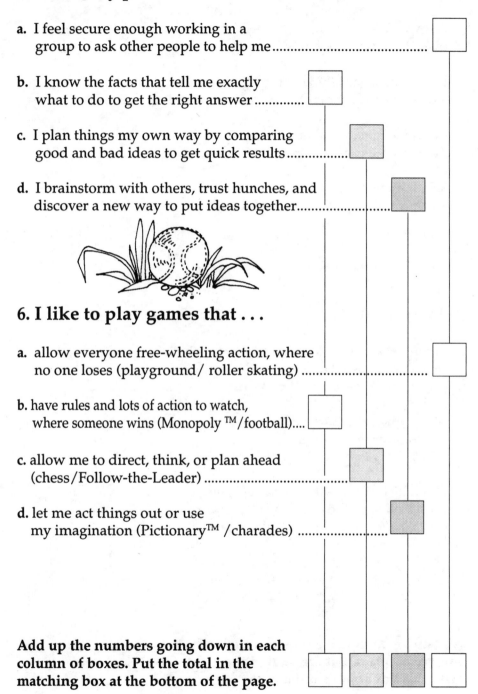

6. I like to play games that . . .

a. allow everyone free-wheeling action, where
no one loses (playground/ roller skating) ....

b. have rules and lots of action to watch,
where someone wins (Monopoly ™/football)....

c. allow me to direct, think, or plan ahead
(chess/Follow-the-Leader) ....

d. let me act things out or use
my imagination (Pictionary™ /charades) ....

**Add up the numbers going down in each
column of boxes. Put the total in the
matching box at the bottom of the page.**

7. I learn best when . . .

a. I can bend the rules in a new way,
discovering things for myself ....

b. I can practice skills I already know
while carefully following instructions ....

c. someone helps me by showing
me the easiest way to get things done ....

d. I can think ideas through, plan, set goals,
and get the job done in my own time ....

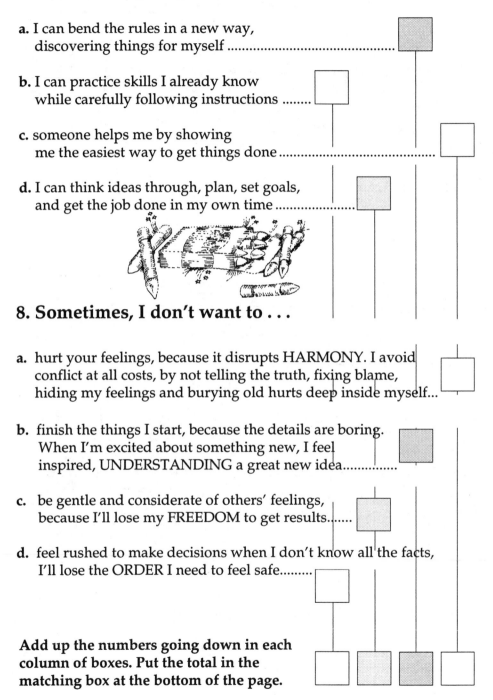

8. Sometimes, I don't want to . . .

a. hurt your feelings, because it disrupts HARMONY. I avoid
conflict at all costs, by not telling the truth, fixing blame,
hiding my feelings and burying old hurts deep inside myself...

b. finish the things I start, because the details are boring.
When I'm excited about something new, I feel
inspired, UNDERSTANDING a great new idea...............

c. be gentle and considerate of others' feelings,
because I'll lose my FREEDOM to get results........

d. feel rushed to make decisions when I don't know all the facts,
I'll lose the ORDER I need to feel safe.........

**Add up the numbers going down in each
column of boxes. Put the total in the
matching box at the bottom of the page.**

Now, let's add up the results.

First, add together the totals in each column on each of the four pages. Enter the numbers in the boxes below.

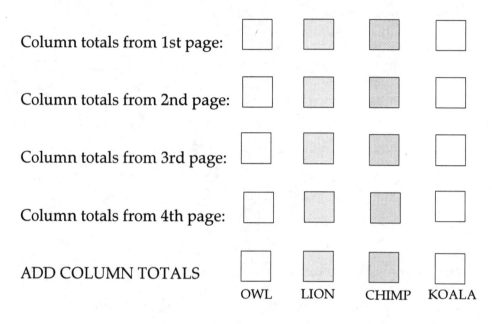

Column totals from 1st page: ☐ ☐ ☐ ☐

Column totals from 2nd page: ☐ ☐ ☐ ☐

Column totals from 3rd page: ☐ ☐ ☐ ☐

Column totals from 4th page: ☐ ☐ ☐ ☐

ADD COLUMN TOTALS ☐ ☐ ☐ ☐

OWL   LION   CHIMP   KOALA

Next, you must divide each COLUMN TOTAL by 2.

For example, if the total in the OWL box is 22, divide 22 by 2 which gives you a new total of 11 ($22 \div 2 = 11$). If the total in the OWL box is 23, the new total would be $11^1/_2$. (Halves are okay!)

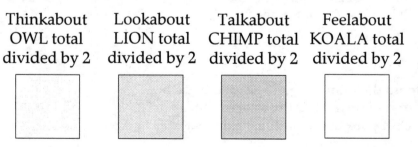

Thinkabout OWL total divided by 2	Lookabout LION total divided by 2	Talkabout CHIMP total divided by 2	Feelabout KOALA total divided by 2
☐	☐	☐	☐

On the next page you'll find the four animals around a tree's growth rings.

On that page, **color** in the same number of growth rings as your final total for each animal.

For example:
If you have 11 as your final Thinkabout Owl total,
color 11 growth rings out from the center
of the tree trunk in the Thinkabout Owl section.

Color the rings of the Thinkabout Owl section grassy green. The orderly Thinkabout part of you is like grass — growing steadily and quietly.

Color the Lookabout Lion section sky blue. The free-spirited Lookabout part of you is like the cool, blue, open, visionary sky.

Color the Talkabout Chimp section sunny yellow. The understanding, Talkabout part of you is like the bright light of the energizing sun.

Color the Feelabout Koala section earthy red. The harmonious Feelabout part of you is like the warm, comforting, friendly earth.

This is the center, or core, of your wholehearted feelings, deeply-rooted values of well-being — the rings of life.

Your SQ Profile

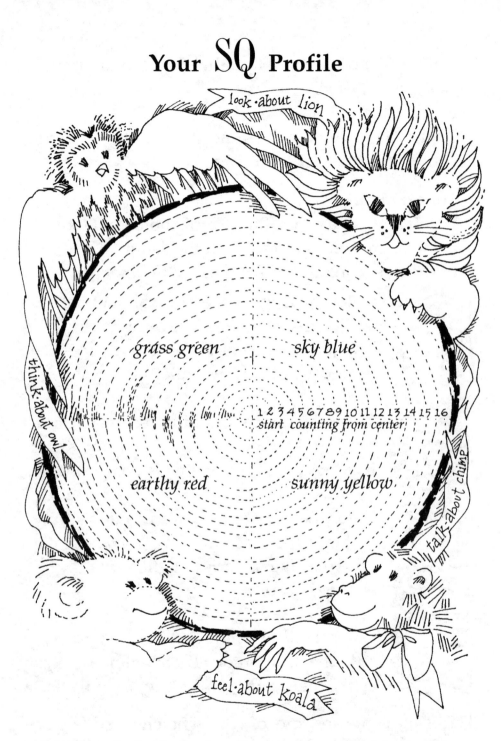

look·about lion

think·about owl

talk·about chimp

feel·about koala

grass green

sky blue

earthy red

sunny yellow

1 2 3 4 5 6 7 8 9 10 11 12 13 14 15 16
start counting from center

Color from the inside out, just the way a tree grows from its heart.

Thinking From The Inside Out

Think-about Owl (Green)

Look-about Lion (Blue)

If you have more green rings, you prefer to think about facts and like to put things in order. You work towards perfection and want the world to be a safe place. You have difficulty expressing your fears, feelings, and opinions without criticizing yourself and others.

If you have more blue rings, you prefer to look around at your surroundings to see how everything could be made better. You prefer to act on a plan rather than a feeling. You like to take charge directing others to get results. You don't accept others' limits of themselves.

If you have more red rings, you prefer to feel about things and use intuition. You are quiet, friendly, and helpful. You like peaceful moments, to feel you belong, and to make things. You have difficulty expressing fear and anger, holding worry inside to avoid losing what is certain and known. No focus means more stress.

If you have more yellow rings, you prefer to talk about ideas first and get reactions. You like to interact and hear how ideas sound. You express excitement, anger, love and want understanding. You like everyone to have fun talking. You feel stress when your motives are misunderstood.

Feel-about Koala (Red)

Talk-about Chimp (Yellow)

Deeply-rooted core values and feelings affect thinking, revealing your natural talents. The section you colored the most rings is your special *inside* self, your *inside* color.

65

a logical grass green

think about owl

feel about koala

an earthy feeling red

66

color the rings

look·about lion

a visionary blue

talk·about chimp

a sunny idea yellow

1 2 3 4 5 6 7 8 9 10 11 12 13 14 15 16

Feelabout Koala and Talkabout Chimp are more intuitive and would rather feel more than think. Thinkabout Owl and Lookabout Lion prefer logical thinking. Thinkabout Owl and Feelabout Koala like a slower pace, waiting for things to happen before they decide, until an idea catches in their minds. They learn by doing things hands-on. Lookabout Lions do things they can get done, and Talkabout Chimps make up their minds quickly, taking risks to create solutions; they tend to grasp the big picture.

Look again at the growth rings you colored. Is one section larger and stronger than the others? Or are they all about the same?

If you are like most people, you have two sections that are stronger. It's important to have strong natural talents, which you recognize and can rely on.

Having really strong natural talents also means you have other talents that you rarely use and may have difficulty understanding, especially in other people. But the whole ring of life is us encircling each other.

On the next page, **outline the appropriate large square** according to green, blue, yellow, or red. For instance, if your strongest section is blue, outline the Look-about square in blue. Then inside this large square, **outline the small square,** with your second strongest color. For example, if your second largest ring is yellow, outline the small Talk-about square inside the large, blue Lookabout square.

Learn to use (or team up with) your less-preferred talents.

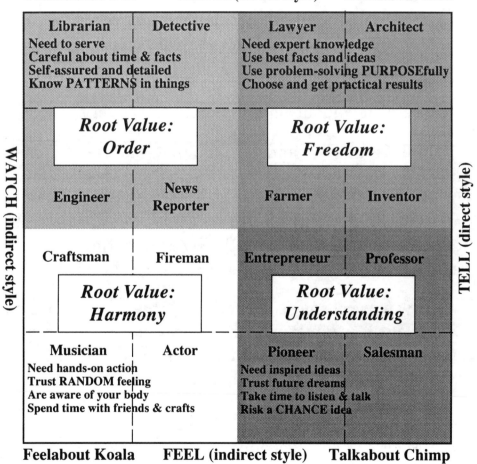

Thinkabout Owl   THINK (direct style)   Lookabout Lion

WATCH (indirect style)

Librarian	Detective	Lawyer	Architect
Need to serve		Need expert knowledge	
Careful about time & facts		Use best facts and ideas	
Self-assured and detailed		Use problem-solving PURPOSEfully	
Know PATTERNS in things		Choose and get practical results	

Root Value: Order

Root Value: Freedom

| Engineer | News Reporter | Farmer | Inventor |

| Craftsman | Fireman | Entrepreneur | Professor |

Root Value: Harmony

Root Value: Understanding

Musician	Actor	Pioneer	Salesman
Need hands-on action		Need inspired ideas	
Trust RANDOM feeling		Trust future dreams	
Are aware of your body		Take time to listen & talk	
Spend time with friends & crafts		Risk a CHANCE idea	

TELL (direct style)

Feelabout Koala   FEEL (indirect style)   Talkabout Chimp

It may seem nice to have a clear path to follow, but an easy well-used path means there is much we may never get to explore. There may even be fences keeping us from traveling beyond our usual path.

We need to *think, see, hear,* and *feel* all of our natural talents, both *inside* and *outside,* so our growth is balanced and our own tree of life grows straight and tall.

The chart on the next page compares our root values and natural talents. It's natural for us to favor one or two talents over others. Notice how the Thinkabout Owl and Look-about Lion prefer *thinking* over *feeling* while Feelabout Koala and Talkabout Chimp prefer *feeling* over *thinking*.

Thinkabout Owl and Feelabout Koala are like each other because they prefer to work on things less urgently in an introverted inside-sort-of-way. Lookabout Lion and Talkabout Chimp are just the opposite. They prefer to express themselves urgently by doing things in an extroverted outside-sort-of-way.

The way we change something in our world depends on which talents we favor and what we pay attention to around us. Changing our minds changes our inner worlds. "We begin to see things as *we* are, not as they are."

Develop your thinking skills for a self-correcting, self aware world. Know that opposites attract so we can learn to work together. Peers matter, so we learn to think anew about things, evolving us all.

Think (direct)

Finish Work Calm Colors Neat	Knowledge Cool Colors Messy
Order, Facts, Safety Think things over, take time, answer questions, listen, and watch.	**Freedom, Choices, Results** Implement plans, make decisions, answer questions, and instruct others.
Action Warm Colors Neat	Inspired Bright Colors Messy
Harmony, Belonging, Activity Feel things, take time, ask questions, and ask others.	Understanding, Ideas, Creativity Take risks, make decisions, answer questions, and create new ideas.

Watch (indirect)

Tell (direct)

Feel (indirect)

On this page, outline one of the four squares that represents your large square. Color your animal's color — green, blue, yellow, or red. You know if your largest growth ring is blue, you outlined the Look-about square in blue.

How does each part of you do what it does best?
We all have lots of different ways of being smart. By
understanding change, we change the world itself.

Think-about Owl, the
Earth Keeper, finds
the right growth way

Look-about Lion, the
Star Leader, shapes
the future way

Feel-about Koala, the
Peace Maker, loves
the easy, active way

Talk-about Chimp, the
Dream Mover, seeks
a new imaginative way

When these close pals team up and work together in
different ways, they show us how to use our unique
strengths to act in the world. When we see how the
whole works, we can achieve much more by working
together — by serving others, leading, taking action,
and growing. New ideas may emerge. If you want to
learn about something, try teaching it to someone else.
No one else learns as much as a teacher.

Rings of Life

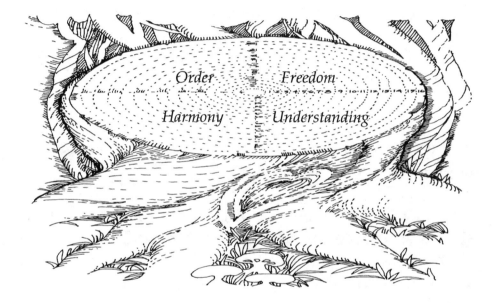

We all need strong roots and good support to stretch and grow, adding new skills on top of previous ones. Our strong roots come from our lasting values — what matters to us most. Each of us experiences life differently. What we have in common is learning how to create new meanings out of good and bad moments. When we do this, we learn to stretch and grow on the *inside* and work and belong together on the *outside*. Thus, we uncover our own true roots and better understand the rings of life.

On the next page, outline the large square with your animal's color — green, blue, yellow, or red.

If your strongest growth ring is blue, outline the large Lookabout square. Then *inside* this large blue square, outline the small square with the color of your second-largest growth ring.

If your second strongest ring is yellow, then outline the small Talkabout square yellow *inside* the large Look-about blue square.

Look at the smaller square you outlined, which shows your second-largest growth ring. Do the characteristics seem familiar and important to you? These are your deeply-rooted values — your emotional core.

We can learn a lot from understanding our deeply-rooted values, as well as others' values. When we feel whole in all four different ways, we understand how thought, experience, and feeling fit together.

The more we learn to interact, we discover happiness comes from the inside out.

	Think Envision Self-Contained Left Brain		
Thinkabout **Owl**			**Lookabout** **Lion**

Researcher facts/facts industrious persistent concerned safekeeping	**Strategic** **Planner** diligent logical outcome organized	**Systems** **Analyst** conceptional vision-logic key issues rational	**Designer** factual definite free from ambiguity critical

— < Facts ——————— Results> ——

Technician disposed to action practical sequential	**Manager** administrative supervise realistic boundaries	**Manufacturer** open-minded to differing points of view	**Program** **Developer** change synthesizer risk-taker

— < Listen ———————— Talk > —

Adventurer facts/ hands-on helpful friendly	**Mechanic** results/hands-on feeling of connection harmonizing	**Entrepreneur** trusting positive simultaneous understanding	**Theorist** integrating beyond wholistic

— < Hands-on ————————— Ideas > —

Artisan passionate feelings deeply involved emotional	**Quality** **Controller** engaged completely common musical	**Pioneer** curious discover flexible respond without effort	**Sales** **Promoter** express effectively exploratory opinion

Logical>   *<Emotional*

Get things done quickly   *Slower to get things done*

Ask Listen Watch Reflect Input   Tell Show Express Output

Feel Create Relate Right Brain			
Feelabout **Koala**			**Talkabout** **Chimp**

When all four senses work together well, something called synergy occurs. When the four Synergy Pals work together to solve problems or achieve tasks, they are truly effective. Interdependence (working together) is always more productive than independence (working alone).

Draw upon the brains of successful people…

We stand on the shoulders of the Great Brains who have come before us, giving us strong roots and good support to stretch and grow, adding new skills to previous ideas. We all need meaningful purpose, leading us to fields of study that interest our common senses. Ecology, quantum physics, mythology, and psychology join our creative global brain, reminding us that peers matter in making our world new again.

Alexander Graham Bell invented the telephone. His influence changed, adapted, and evolved us for today's technology culture. Find a Great Brain style like yours.

Smarter Together
Turn Conflict into Cooperation

"Do
unto others
as they'd like
done unto them"
Tony Alessandra

Whole Mind, Happy Heart

GREEN | BLUE

GREEN

I Need Time to Figure It Out
I Feel
Cornered and Stubborn
When
You push or criticize me
Because
I Value Order and Conformity
I Need a quiet, safe place
Lesson:
RISK starting without a plan, rules or all the facts
SHARE my feelings and be kind
STRETCH my boundaries for just having fun.
I am contemplative at my best, critical at my worst

ORDER

THINKABOUT OWL

BLUE

I Need To Act on Plans & Direct
I Feel
Blocked
When
You avoid decision and follow-through action
Because
I Value Freedom to act
I Need to do new things and get Results
Lesson:
RISK being fun-loving & work more slowly
SHARE and listen to *your* feelings, as well as words
STRETCH to be considerate and accept what others offer. At my best, decisive, defiant at my worst

FREEDOM

LOOKABOUT LION

FEELABOUT KOALA | TALKABOUT CHIMP

I Need to Be Part of the Group
I Feel
Left Out
When
What I feel doesn't seem to matter
Because
I Value Harmony
Need to be part of what's going on
Lesson:
RISK being honest about my needs and feelings
SHARE *my* decisions, expectations and dreams
STRETCH to challenge myself and take charge
I provide good service at my best, lazy at my worst

HARMONY

RED

I Need to Question and Communicate
I Feel
Misunderstood
When
You don't listen to my inspired ideas or share my playful mood
Because
I Value Understanding
I Need to direct myself and Question the rules
Lesson:
RISK losing inspiration by too much organization
SHARE the work
STRETCH to plan ahead, work with enthusiasm, my best, unfocused at my worst

UNDERSTANDING

YELLOW

Talkabout Chimp Understands

Feeling needs are
satisfied with

Understanding
Ideas
Creativity

"Let me tell you about this fantastic new idea.
Tell me what you think of it."

Talkabout Chimp's Pals say:

Let's play with it and see what happens if we do it differently.

Given what we know is true, it's possible that . . .

Let's find out what's on the other side of that mountain.

Talkabout Chimp is matter-of-fact. . .

. . . with the Thinkabout Owl pal

I do just what you want me to when you're at home with me because I share the need with you for a happy family. And as I grow, we share ideals I never want to lose. Sometimes I bend the rules, when our ideas defuse. Thinkabout, expects details of me; some rules are much too rash and should be left in school.

What Hurts?
Name the Trouble

I retreat at times from your step-by-step tasks. It takes risk and courage to think outside the box. Walks and talks will make it clear, my dream is bigger than your fear, as we stumble thru some mental blocks.

Talkabout Chimp takes risks. . .

. . . with the
Lookabout
Lion
pal

My feelings go so very deep. I strive for your affection. You keep your mind so far away. I don't get much attention. I always want to talk to you about the dreams I feel. I cannot seem to find a way to make my magic real. You want me to be perfect in everything I do. I find it just impossible to please the perfect you.

What Hurts?
Name the Trouble

Everything is a logical vision to you before it's real. To me the thing that makes good sense, are inspired ideas I feel. Vision makes us both click so ideas and plans seem real. Action is our measuring stick.

Talkabout Chimp uses playfulness . . .

. . . with the Feelabout Koala pal

You like to play in new and fun-filled ways. In action or in traction many days. Although I know just how you feel I'm not one to compete. Better angels of our nature chase gloom if we chance to meet. Scary doubts endured in brainy groups become our discovery shouts.

What Hurts?
Name the Trouble

Scolding you for heading south I feel alone and sad. When you never say how brave I am, I truly do feel bad. Showing off on some cool craft, you risk some laughs to feel glad. Acting daft in a motion poster, brave stunts you never fake. Cuz' joy rides on your emotional roller coaster when your belonging is at stake.

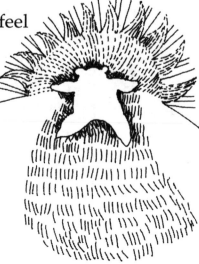

Talkabout Chimp jump-starts new understanding...

...with the
Talkabout
Chimp
pal

Creating well with others, how nice to be with you. We walk and talk together lots of times; we're sensitive and true. Hearing the call for us is the same. Finding meaning in the seeking is our idea game. Discovering new ways to help our Earth Mother, we remember and learn with each other.

What Hurts:
Name the Trouble

Perhaps what I'm about to say you couldn't have suspected. Exchanging bright ideas that go nowhere, my soul feels quite neglected. You're busy pleasing others, please help the brainstorm starter. A smart move brings us finishers, to help us all work smarter.

How to work with the Synthesis Learner. . .

Talkabout Chimp

Values = Understanding and Fun

- Learns by reorganizing
- Many good answers
- Judges by these standards:
  Is it original?
  Is it formally coherent?
  Is it expressive?

Tips for Caregivers

How to Best Help a Talkabout Chimp

- Promote their ideas
- Be a resource
- Become an evaluator
- Serve as facilitator
- Encourage innovation
- Let them explain
- Be the storyteller

create...what if...?
...is like a...because...
showcase...

Talkabout Chimp Student

I love to share my
far-out thoughts, to
speak out and have
fun. You'll find me
in the spotlight
before the day is done.
It's hard for me to fit
myself into a routine pace.
But please respect my feelings. I need
unstructured space.

Talkabout Chimp Teacher

I love to be creative, to watch my students grow.

I bring excitement to the class. The magic
starts to show. My
approach is quite
unstructured.
Unpredictable,
as well. Make believe,
democracy — To teach
these things is swell.

Talkabout Chimp says:
"I'm quick to anger, fast to talk, because the words are real. I sense injustice, moral outrage, about the pain I feel. I'm not unfair, nor shun the risk.

For when the upset's over
an outrageous story
inspires — lots of
ideas courageous —
from brave lessons
we perspire.
No matter how
hilarious, a story
is a promise, mad, sad,
glad, or ominous.

Talkabout Chimp
is an idea starter

When I'm threatened, I may act . . .	I need to learn how to . . .
Scattered	Organize details
Let-down	Follow through, focus
Overwhelmed	Plan ahead
Pushy	Listen to others
Naïve	Be practical
Worried	Delegate jobs
. . . because I feel bad.	. . . to feel good.

When I Am a Talkabout Chimp
I Need to Question and Communicate

I FEEL	Misunderstood
WHEN	Others don't listen to my inspired ideas or share my playful mood
BECAUSE	I value understanding and I need to direct myself and seek new rules
I MUST RISK	Losing inspiration to be organized
AND SHARE	The work that can be delegated
AND STRETCH	To plan ahead and finish step by step

88

If Your Heart Could Talk
About Understanding

Save Talkabout Chimp From a

Heartache

By **UNDERSTANDING** How to
Create Ideas in a New and Fun Way

Heartlight

A little change of heart can be the biggest change of all.

Match and Mismatch
with Talkabout Chimp

Lookabout's....with Talkabout
THEY MISMATCH HERE... Impatient
THEY MATCH HERE... Vision Quest

Feelabout's... with Talkabout
THEY MISMATCH HERE...FollowThrough
THEY MATCH HERE...Listens to my ideas

Thinkabout's... with Talkabout
THEY MISMATCH HERE... Pessimistic
THEY MATCH HERE...Search for Answers

Talkabout's... with Talkabout
THEY MISMATCH HERE...Impulse control
THEY MATCH HERE...Optimistic Dreamer

Mark X on the line...how you feel you really are
when life goes exactly as you've planned it.
It's the match that counts...
when we work smarter together

Routine...............................or.............................Original
Expressive..........................or.............................Reflective
FollowThrough.................or.............................Initiating
Exacting.............................or.........................Spontaneous

90

Thinkabout Owl
Order

Feeling needs are
satisfied with

Order
Facts
Safety

*"Once we get all the facts in order,
we'll know the best way to do things."*

Thinkabout Owl's pals say:

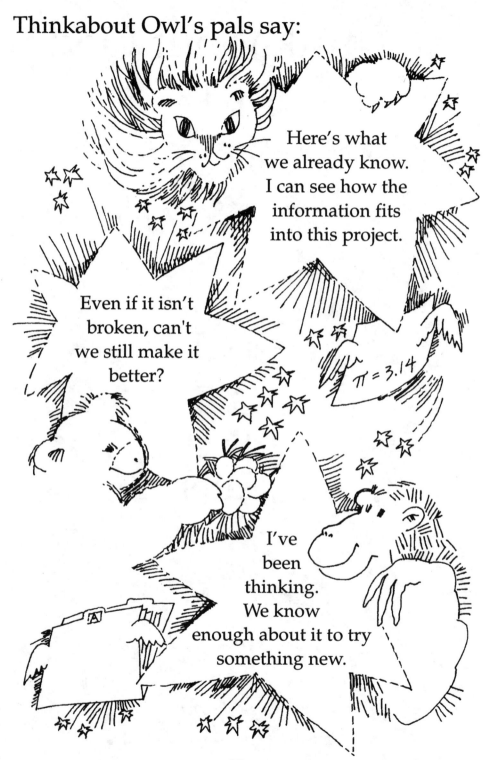

Here's what we already know. I can see how the information fits into this project.

Even if it isn't broken, can't we still make it better?

$\pi = 3.14$

I've been thinking. We know enough about it to try something new.

Thinkabout Owl finds order when we need it...

...with the Thinkabout Owl pal

Our relationship is brilliant. We support each other well. We both enjoy the rules of home; all the order is just swell. The tradition of our family tree brightens up our life. Stability, we do agree, brings comfort without strife.

What Hurts?
Name the Trouble

We get along so very well, there are rules we always see. We work too hard much of the time. Parties can set us free. To finish we must our details share. Because it's right and you really do care.

Thinkabout Owl is a cool onlooker. . .

. . . with the
Feel-about
Koala pal

I love tradition, plans, ideas.
For me these are my tools.
But you give no direction;
you have too few rules.
You love your fun,
and that's okay, but I
like order, please. In
action or in traction is
your way. Stability
remember, brings
me ease.

What Hurts?
Name the Trouble

I'm embarrassed
by disorder. I'm not
your laundry sorter.
You clutter up my
need for certainty and
don't think problems to the
end, no exit strategy. So off you
go leaving me to fend. However, a
helping hand you sometimes lend,
flexible as a noodle you always bend.

Thinkabout Owl gets to the point at a steady pace . . .

. . . with the Lookabout Lion pal

You're way off in the future. I need you here and now.
I want some ordered guidance. I'd love to know just
how. I know you have big dreams for me that I hope I
can fulfill. But you're a bit demanding.
Please see that, if you will.

What Hurts?
Name the Trouble

If I am to fulfill my
dreams, if I'm allowed to
shine, I need a bit more detail
how I will use my time. I need to know
more numbers, then we'll focus fine.
Gather, manage, use this info in a web or a line.

Thinkabout Owl challenges risky ideas. . .

. . . with the
Talkabout
Chimp
pal

Our family needs a more sensible rule. A "backbone," an outline; that would be super cool. Your mind goes to things that are not very real. My mind wants a structure to touch and to feel. We do like to help other people, that's true. Getting along is our song, cuz we're both true blue.

What Hurts?
Name the Trouble

I have a deep need for a practical way to direct my whole life, to plan every day. You're too idealistic. I cannot compare. Your head is in the clouds, way off somewhere.

How to work with the Fact Finder...

Thinkabout Owl

Values = Order and Safety

- Learns by remembering
    (facts, definitions, steps in a procedure)
- Answers are always clear and easy to check
- Judges self and others by correctness

Tips for Caregivers

How to Best Help a Thinkabout Owl

- Show them how they are right
- Provide information through direct instruction
- Use knowledge to increase comprehension
- Break work into steps

List...Define...
Who, what, where,
when, how, why...

Thinkabout Owl Student

I love my school, respect its rules. I need routine and order. I'm punctual, dependable. You know I am a learner. I share in all the duties that I'm told we all should do. I want our subjects plainly taught. I need to hear from you.

Thinkabout Owl Teacher

My teaching style is clearly geared toward order and routine. I am consistent in my way. My students are a team. I teach them what our country stands for, the duties we all share. I discipline when necessary. I know I'm firm and fair.

Thinkabout Owl says:

"I'm very slow to anger. I really have no buffer. I criticize and blame myself, spin my wheels and suffer. I'm stubborn when I'm cornered. I feel stuck in the mud until I pick up my poor self and step out with a thud."

Thinkabout Owl
is a caretaker

When threatened, **I may act . . .**	**I need to learn** **how to . . .**
Aloof	Express my feelings
Picky	Be spontaneous
Deliberate	Just get started
Bored	Enjoy unstructured time
Stubborn	Get along with active people
Suspicious	Trust others' decisions
. . . because I feel bad.	**. . . to feel good.**

When I am a Thinkabout Owl
I Need Time to Figure it Out

I FEEL	Cornered and stubborn
WHEN	Others push or criticize me
BECAUSE	I value order and conformity. I need a quiet, safe place to work and play.
I MUST RISK	Starting without rules in order to be creative
AND SHARE	My feelings and be kind
AND STRETCH	My boundaries for having fun

100

If Your Heart Could Talk
About Order

Save Thinkabout Owl From Being

Heartless

Needs **ORDER** Doing Things
the Right and Safe Way

Openheart

A little change of heart can be the biggest change of all.

Match and Mismatch
with Thinkabout Owl

Lookabout's....with Thinkabout's
THEY MISMATCH HERE... Impatience
THEY MATCH HERE... Goal Completion

Feelabout's... with Thinkabout's
THEY MISMATCH HERE...Leisurely
THEY MATCH HERE... Harmony

Thinkabout's... with Thinkabout's
THEY MISMATCH HERE... Being Right
THEY MATCH HERE...Practice Carefully

Talkabout ... with Thinkabout's
THEY MISMATCH HERE...Relishes Change
THEY MATCH HERE...Likes Being Direct

Mark X on the line...how do you feel
when life goes exactly as you've planned it.
It's the match that counts...
when we work smarter together.

Right ....or......................... Risk taker
Quiet.............................or....................................Noisy
Focused.........................or............................Unplanned
Finisher.........................or.................................Starter

Lookabout Lion
Freedom

Feeling needs are
satisfied with

Freedom
Choices
Results

*"We'll get somewhere only if we choose what
we want to have happen."*

Lookabout Lion's pals say:

I've carefully looked at the problem overall. Here's what we can do.

Let's make a model to see if the material will work.

I understand what we're trying to do. There may be more than one way to do it.

Lookabout Lion plans things...

... with the Talkabout Chimp pal

I need to be my own true self, much different from your own. We live in worlds not quite alike. I'm distant and alone. While you enjoy the family ties, I take off by myself. My mind quests for new knowledge from the books upon the shelf.

What Hurts?
Name the Trouble

There are times when I feel smothered by your need to talk and talk. You show too much emotion; you make me want to walk. To get things done we walk and talk. This is what I need—to grow into the person who is me, at my own speed.

Lookabout Lion finds new plans . . .

. . . with the
Thinkabout
Owl pal

I try to find a place we match, but all we do, it seems, is clash.
The family is dear to you; planning for the future, too. What
you seem to want for me is safety and security. But the thing I
love to do is search and search to find a clue, to bring an
unknown thought to view.

What Hurts?
Name the Trouble

I'm very independent.
I act on what I know. I ask
you, please, to do the work.
Please come along or watch me search
and grow. Invent a way to be abstract,
for something new to come today.

106

Lookabout Lion designs models. . .

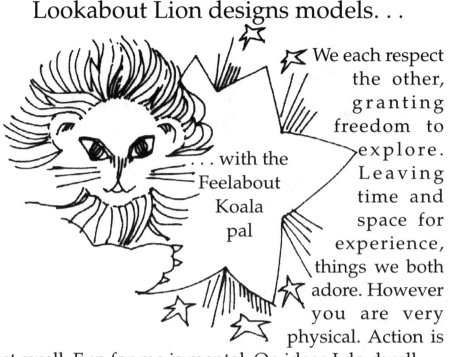

We each respect the other, granting freedom to explore. Leaving time and space for experience, things we both adore. However you are very physical. Action is just swell. Fun for me is mental. On ideas I do dwell.

. . . with the Feelabout Koala pal

What Hurts?
Name the Trouble

You live in the now, I 'm future focused, on this we do agree. You are so clever as everyone can see, the coolest thing in leather. My mind lives out somewhere in space , above the boundless blue, missing your ol' smiling face.

Lookabout Lion is a freedom fighter. . .

. . . with the Lookabout Lion pal

We are, after all, alike. We love to be inventive. Our wisdom shines, our vision-logic grows. At times we're quite selective. We're distant with each other because we're independent. Yet we can cheer each other on, to be quite resplendent.

What Hurts?
Name the Trouble

We are both quite powerful and very much alike. Generation gaps can cause a rift, as we clash in cycles of our life. I want to be as strong as you, but you're the one in charge. So, it seems, we do compete in matters small and large.

How to work with the Confident Learner...

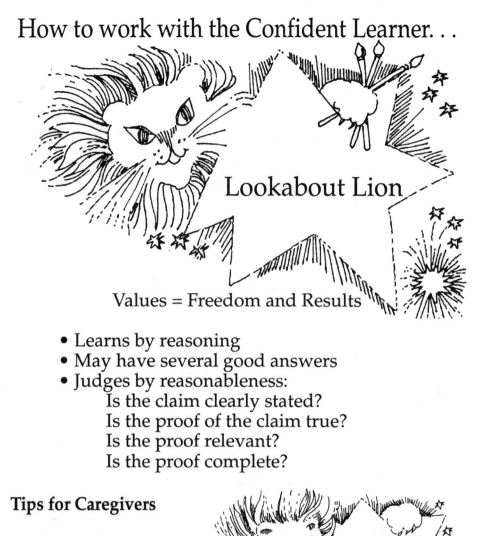

Lookabout Lion

Values = Freedom and Results

- Learns by reasoning
- May have several good answers
- Judges by reasonableness:
    Is the claim clearly stated?
    Is the proof of the claim true?
    Is the proof relevant?
    Is the proof complete?

Tips for Caregivers

How to Best Help a
Lookabout Lion

Ask for cause
and effects
Compare and contrast
Prove the
statement...

- Give them slack
- Become a coach
- Build models
- Involve the student
- Give immediate feedback
- Provide the freedom to act

$\pi = 3.14$

Lookabout Lion Student

I love to look inside a thought to see just how it works. I love to work all by myself to find out all the quirks. I'm logical, I'm curious, I need to understand. It makes me happy when you tell me just how good I am.

Lookabout Lion Teacher

I seek to answer nature's riddles, and help you do the same. To give you useful information is my highest aim. I inspire you to stretch your mind, to find an answer rare. I create new ways of teaching you. I really, truly care.

Lookabout Lion Says:
"I'm quick to anger — step aside!
My fury is volcanic. I tend to zap the calmer one,
and this can make you panic, but then it's over and
forgotten. I'm on to other things. If you can move
along with me, accomplishment this brings."

Lookabout Lion — a born leader

When I'm threatened **I may act . . .**	**I need to learn** **how to . . .**
Bossy	Be less demanding
Blunt	Consider others' needs
Unfeeling	Listen to feelings
Serious	Be more fun and creative
Demanding	Relax and slow down
Like I "know it all"	Poke fun at myself
	Laugh with others
. . . because I feel bad.	**. . . to feel good.**

When I am a Lookabout Lion
I Need to act on Plans, to Direct

I FEEL	Blocked
WHEN	Others avoid decision and follow-through to finish tasks
BECAUSE	I value freedom to act and I need to do new things and get results
I MUST RISK	Working more slowly in order to be fun-loving and considerate
AND SHARE	And listen to others' feelings and words
AND STRETCH	To be considerate and accept what others offer, to enjoy each other.

112

If Your Heart Could TalkAbout Freedom

Save Lookabout Lion From Being

Hardhearted

Needs **FREEDOM**
For Doing Things My Own Way

Braveheart

A little change of heart can be the biggest change of all.

Match and Mismatch
with Lookabout Lion

 ## Lookabout's....with Lookabout Lion
THEY MISMATCH HERE... Boastful
THEY MATCH HERE... Self-Confident

 ## Feelabout's... with Lookabout Lion
THEY MISMATCH HERE...Sensitive
THEY MATCH HERE... Adventurous

 ## Thinkabout's... with Lookabout Lion
THEY MISMATCH HERE... Action
THEY MATCH HERE...Tasks Well done

 ## Talkabout ... with Lookabout Lion
THEY MISMATCH HERE...Neglected
THEY MATCH HERE...Ingenious

Mark, X on the line...how do you feel
when life goes exactly as you've planned it.
It's the match that counts...
when we work smarter together

Self-Assured.........................or.......................Fun-Loving
Act Boldly............................or............................Cautious
Direct....................................or...........................Amiable
Challenged............................or...............................Careful

Feelabout Koala Harmony

Feeling needs are
satisfied by

Harmony
Belonging
Hands-On

"I made it just for you.
I knew you'd like it."

Feelabout Koala's pals say:

You have to handle
things with just
the force required.
Not more
or less.

We can
build it
together
if we all
lend a
hand.

It's okay the
way it is, but let's
move a few
things
around a little.
It won't hurt it.

Feelabout Koala is fun in action ...

... with the Thinkabout Owl pal

We do not get along at all. Our values disagree. I like to take a risk or two in spontaneity. But you want things to stay the same, predictability. You are very ordered. It's either right or wrong. You see, I'm quite impulsive. I want it fast. I'm strong.

What Hurts?
Name the Trouble

I like to have a lot of fun. I fire, get ready, then aim. You aim, get ready and never fire liking everything the same. "No rules" might mean disorder. If we start out easy, would you come along and be my useful porter? I like to make the jump, take the risk, you do not. We know each other's skills can be taught.

Feelabout Koala finds the easy ways. . .

. . . with the Lookabout Lion pal

We both are very competent. We both are quite direct. We both know that we do compete, but you want to protect. Your mind seems very far away leading future goals and dreams. So, we don't always get along. I love the here and now of teams. I love to play and hide. Hard work you'd rather have me do brings me no joy inside.

What Hurts?
Name the Trouble

Oftentimes, my feelings ache. I don't feel good enough. You want me to be picture perfect, and that is really tough. Turn tasks into fun with my handy skills. Understanding how we like to work is really not so rough. Imagine my hands-on with your heads-up we could have many thrills.

Feelabout Koala boosts others. . .

. . . with the
Talkabout
Chimp
pal

I know you understand that I'm my own person. Encourage me to explore ideas, and seek some brand new fun. I need to have some guidelines. You allow me to play the fool. And then you want to know too much of what I think and do. I'm very independent, as you already know. Your think tank interact is when I get away and go.

What Hurts?
Name the Trouble

Responsible I am for everything I do, but when, at times, I ask for help, you do not follow through. Don't lose your sunny smiling face. Just change the message so the rest of us can understand. First at the gate is hard to replace for your too fortune cookie fans?

Feel-about Koala finds harmony...

...with the Feelabout Koala pal

The time we spend together is a pleasure to us both. We are so very active, our energies just flow. Compatible together we know each other's needs. You're really bold. Craving great excitement, I'd even say courageous. Yes, speed ahead indeed, cuz we're just a bit outrageous.

What Hurts?
Name the Trouble
I like your free-wheeling attitude, clever pluck. We love to be together on adventures that bring luck, cool and clever never rude. Very scary to be at odds. We understand each other, ready, fire, duck. Cuz we're fighting our own mod squad.

How to work with the Teamwork Learner. . .

Feelabout Koala

Values = Harmony and Cooperation

• Learns by relating
• Answers are easily checked, often by peers
• Judges by these standards:
• Does the answer demonstrate that the
• Student knows him/herself and others?
• Harmony: a value with cooperation, charms others

Tips for Caregivers

How to best help a Feelabout Koala

• Show how they are liked
• Focus their high energy, enthusiasm
• Use the discussion approach
• Be a motivator
• Bond through activities
• Build follow-through
• Organize
• Prioritize

Which do you prefer? If you were in this situation, what would you do?

Feelabout
Koala Student

I am impulsive and physical. I want a lot of action. I make good use of what I learn. I like the competition. I learn by doing with my hands. I love to work with tools. When conflicts come, though, I withdraw. Fighting is for fools.

Feelabout
Koala Teacher

The information that I teach is useful here and now. I do not plan, but what I do excites each one--and how! My teaching style's dynamic. I act quickly when I must. I have rapport, and lots of joy. I'm one that you can trust.

Feelabout Koala says:
"I find it rather difficult to let hurt feelings show.
I'm very easy-going, so you would never know.
I keep it all pent up inside till I can hold no more.
Then please watch out! I may just shout,
To act on what I've stored."

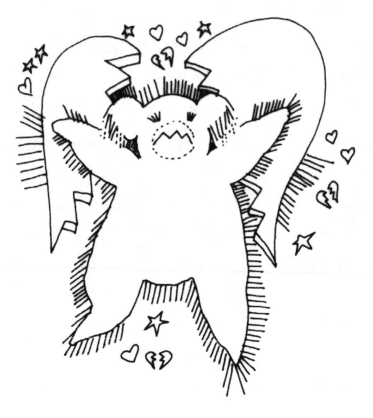

Feelabout Koala — a shaker and mover

When threatened, I may act . . .	**I need to learn how to . . .**
Lonely	Be independent
Afraid	Be honest about feelings
Gullible	Be assertive
Sneaky	Be confident
Guilty	Do good work
Impulsive	Know my boundaries

. . . because I feel bad.   **. . . to feel good.**

When I Am a Feelabout Koala
I Need to Be a Part of the Group

I FEEL	Left out
WHEN	What I feel and do doesn't seem to matter
BECAUSE	I value harmony and I need to be a part of what's going on
I MUST RISK	Being honest about my needs in order to start and finish tasks
AND SHARE	My decisions, expectations, and boundaries
AND STRETCH	Myself to lead and risk failure

If Your Heart Could Talk
About Harmony

Save Feelabout Koala From a

Heavyheart

Needs **HARMONY**
For Doing Things Easily Together

Happyheart

A little change of heart can be the biggest change of all.

Match and Mismatch
with Feelabout Koala

Lookabout's....with Feelabout Koala
THEY MISMATCH HERE... Self-Discipline
THEY MATCH HERE... Self-Confident

Feelabout's... with Feelabout Koala
THEY MISMATCH HERE...Unfocused
THEY MATCH HERE... Dramatic

Thinkabout's... with Feelabout Koala
THEY MISMATCH HERE... Disorder
THEY MATCH HERE...Devoted

Talkabout ... with Feelabout Koala
THEY MISMATCH HERE...Indirect
THEY MATCH HERE...Cooperative

Mark X on the line...how do you feel
when life goes exactly as you've planned it.
It's the match that counts...
when we work smarter together.

Routine.......................... or .... Exacting
Self Sacrificing ....or .... Self Preservation
Careful...........................or .... Rule Bender
Realistic ....or .... Spontaneous

Friendly Universe

Talkabout Chimp, Thinkabout Owl, Lookabout Lion, and Feelabout Koala learn lots when they understand each other's feelings. It really is healing, seeing each as part of the whole. Becoming whole from the inside out is a light. The Synergy Pals show us a love of what's right.

When we know all the troubles and face them, we're brave. We know all the monsters inside. They come from the fears that all of us have, though we express them differently outside. We're afraid we'll never feel loved. We may feel rejected, neglected or misunderstood. We might become mixed up on "could," "would," and "should."

Our gifts they are many, whether we be short or tall.
Yet in the Friendly Universe, kindness is the finest gift of all.

English

Tomorrow when school is out, I plan to buy a little pumpkin for myself.

1970 October   Peter

This is my son Peter, strategically planning when he was eight. Now he plans virtual tunnels very well.

Growing Seasons

Are you a tiny tree with a lot of growing to do? Or have you grown a lot already? How many oak trees are there in an acorn?

Although we can never completely know and understand another person's ideas and experiences, we can all increase our awareness of the differences. Learn to be thankful of life within, around and beyond you.

What is not Synergistic

Too much sameness = no creative action
Too much difference = no agreement
Too much misdirected natural talent = burnout
Undeveloped natural talents = anger, tension, strain

What's on your mind? think, look, talk, feel
1. I can accept that there are unknowns in life.

Choices — I know I can be myself and make up my mind independently, even if I'm different from others.

Disappointments — I can feel okay, even if I don't always understand what's going on around me. I can learn by looking at my mistakes.

Relationships — I can accept other people the way they are, without needing to put them down. I can appreciate our natural differences.

In my mind's eye I think that good things will happen. Is It More Me or Someone Else?

If I'm scared of unknowns, who makes me feel better?

Me •————•————•————•————•————• Someone else

When I'm feeling okay, who makes me feel scared about unknowns?

Me •————•————•————•————•————• Someone else

Who is in control of changing how I think and feel?

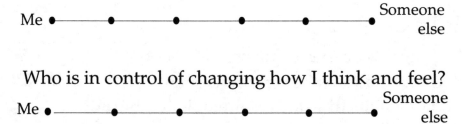

Me •————•————•————•————•————• Someone else

130

These are the unknowns I can accept in my life:

_____

_____

_____

_____

_____

2. I can stay open to new information and ideas.

Choices — I can change my opinion, given new information. I can consider new ideas and treat them as possibilities.

Disappointments — I can admit my misjudgements, readjust, and allow others to do the same.

Relationships — I'm willing to listen to what others have to say. I don't need to make others agree with me.

I can bounce back and learn "aha's" from my mistakes. Is It More Me or Someone Else?

Who helps me stay open to new ideas when others don't understand my dreams?

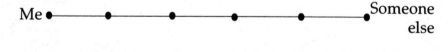

Me •——•——•——•——•Someone
                                else

When I'm feeling okay, who makes me feel worse about ideas?

Me •——•——•——•——•Someone
                                else

Who is in control of how I think and feel?

Me •——•——•——•——•Someone
                                else

Information and idea collaborators in my life are…

_____

_____

_____

_____

_____

3. **I can talk about what hurts, in order to be helpful, instead of repressing my words and thoughts.**

    Choices — I can choose my words and tone of voice to really communicate and say what I mean.

    Disappointments — I can expand my range of expression so that others can understand my words better. I can learn from others' misunderstandings.

    Relationships — I can listen to and respect what others are trying to say to me. I can understand that there are different expressions and perceptions.

I reach out to someone who needs comfort.
Is It More Me or Someone Else?

Who helps me decide when it's safe to talk about what hurts?

Me •————•————•————•————•————• Someone else

When I'm feeling okay, who makes me feel worse, feel accepted?

Me •————•————•————•————•————• Someone else

Who is in control of how I think and feel?

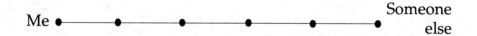

Me •————•————•————•————•————• Someone else

Helpers I've helped and what I've done...

_____

_____

_____

_____

_____

4. I can choose to see the good side of things.

Choices — I can be creative in life and look for opportunities.

Disappointments — I can accept that bad things happen to good people. I can learn to look for meaning.

Relationships — I can choose to see the good side of others and myself.

I will look closely at a flower or tree I haven't noticed before. Is It More Me or Someone Else?

Who helps me see the good side of things, even when I'm disappointed?

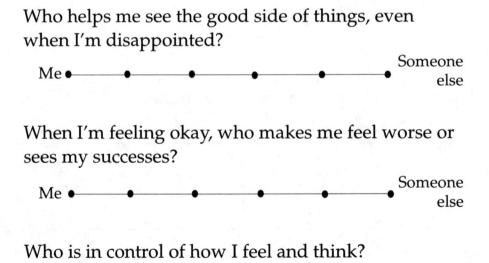

Me ●————●————●————●————●———● Someone else

When I'm feeling okay, who makes me feel worse or sees my successes?

Me ●————●————●————●————●———● Someone else

Who is in control of how I feel and think?

Me ●————●————●————●————●———● Someone else

The good things in my life now are...

_____

_____

_____

_____

_____

5. I can choose to see the funny side of life.

Choices —I can choose to see life's experiences as an amusing story.

Disappointments — With a sense of humor, I can learn to see the funny side of my setback.

Relationships — I can laugh and learn from my own experiences, and laugh with — not at — others.

Be patient with an annoying person, by believing you can make things better with laughter.
Is A Sense of Humor More Me or Someone Else?

Who helps me see the funny side of things?

Me ●———●———●———●———●———● Someone else

When I'm feeling okay, who makes me feel worse or makes me laugh?

Me ●———●———●———●———●———● Someone else

Who is in control of how I think and feel?

Me ●———●———●———●———●———● Someone else

Funny friends and fun things in my life now are...

_____

_____

_____

_____

6. I can choose to look at details without losing sight of the big picture or plan.

Choices — I can seek out information step by step, to solve problems in unusual and creative ways.

Disappointments — I can learn a lot from acting too quickly on a project that I don't know how to finish.

Relationships — I can understand the benefits of synergy — working with others who have different talents than I do.

Do something special for yourself. Focus deeply on each detail. Is It More Me or Someone Else?

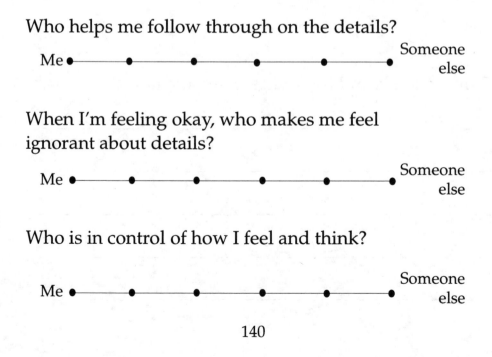

Who helps me follow through on the details?

Me ●——————●——————●——————●——————●——————● Someone else

When I'm feeling okay, who makes me feel ignorant about details?

Me ●——————●——————●——————●——————●——————● Someone else

Who is in control of how I feel and think?

Me ●——————●——————●——————●——————●——————● Someone else

First things first, priority details in my life now are…

_____

_____

_____

_____

_____

7. I can accept my own truth while looking at my surroundings with an open mind.

Choices — I can do what I think is right, not just what others want me to do. I can look at other ways of doing things and choose to be courageous.

Disappointments — I can take pleasure in learning something important, instead of letting fear drive me away.

Relationships — I can set my own boundaries and take care of myself when others do things I don't want to do. I can become more self-reliant and depend on myself. We discover we are as happy as we make up our mind to be. What's on your mind? You are what you think.

"What is mind? no matter. What is matter? Never mind." Is It More Me or Someone Else?

Who helps me see my own true cycles of growth?

Me ●————●————●————●————● Someone else

When I'm feeling okay, who makes me feel worse or okay about what's true for me?

Me ●————●————●————●————● Someone else

Who is in control of how I think and feel?

Me ●————●————●————●————● Someone else

New truths I'm taking control of in my life are...

_____

_____

_____

_____

_____

The Gaps of Give and Take
● How We Differ ● Where do you stand on the line? ●

1. Starting from the center dot, mark an X along the line where you feel in control of your own expectations.
2. Mark a √ on what *other* people expect of you.
3. Draw a line between the X, your expectations, and the √, others' expectations of you.
4. Too much safety or too little risk-taking.

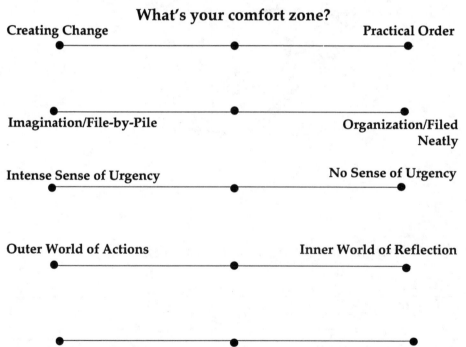

I Prefer/I Feel: X ● ● ● ● ● ● ● ● ● ● ● Others Expect: √ We Differ

What's your comfort zone?

Creating Change   Practical Order

Imagination/File-by-Pile   Organization/Filed Neatly

Intense Sense of Urgency   No Sense of Urgency

Outer World of Actions   Inner World of Reflection

Dreams of Possibilities   A Plan for Precise Work

The length of the line between the X and the √ shows how different expectations can be. A short line means you adapt to change easily. With a longer line, you need to be gently guided or take small steps in order to stem fears. Understanding differences and how they make a good fit together, will change your thinking, feelings, and behavior.

Change the Way You Think About the World

Now I can understand myself and others. Without you there's no us. It's in the struggle to be alive to know how we like to do things and work together. We all fit together in The Synergy Tree of Life.

Change is okay too, when I understand myself. I'm not afraid to learn new things, to wonder, wander, stumble, and grow. It's perfectly all right to do something different. If I get into trouble, I know I always have a safe place within, beyond and around me. My Synergy Pals will always be there as guides. We can think about how the struggle and joy of working and belonging together is the wonder of life.

I understand my friends, "myself in everyone" too, because I see a bit of myself in everyone. That makes my journey through life an interesting trip. Our journey together holds love's promise of becoming a new whole me and you from the inside out.

All about me and all about you, the Friendly Universe nourishes and encourages us. Order, freedom, understanding, and harmony encircle each other in the Friendly Universe, and it continues on and on...

145

"*The trees in the street are old trees used to living with people, family trees that remember your grandfather's name.*"
Anonymous Child

Four Synergy Trees

We are all branches on the synergy trees. A tree reaches for light and grows. The whole world is this tree of life —— reaching for the light of deeper understanding.

Old roots and new rules tell us that we need to learn how to work together to grow whole. The resources of the world bring this process into focus. The core of who you are as a person is what your passion is all about. Real freedom is believing in yourself.

Being true to our nature, while living in the roots of our life, brings joy.

148

The Talkabout Chimp Inspires Ideas

Talkabout Chimps are right-brained and love new ideas. They prefer hunches over logic. They are called *auditory* people because they respond to tone of voice and like to hear how ideas sound. They like warm, bright colors, and bold combinations.

The Talkabout Chimp is the Dream Mover

Talkabouts communicate things — ideas, creations, inspirations, and questions. Talkabouts like to talk about their ideas so others will respond. They love to be inspired. Talkabouts like to learn on their own, question the rules, take risks, and try new things. Talkabouts are messy people. They file by pile. They want to be understood and understand why people believe and act as they do. They are creative problem-solvers; they like to do things a new way. They look on the bright side, their glass is half full, (not half empty). When Talkabouts are excited,  angry, or loving, everyone within earshot knows. Feeling they're not understood can cause Talkabouts stress. They can be resentful, worried, depressed, and not follow through on commitments.

The Thinkabout Owl Practices Carefully

Thinkabout Owls are left-brained and love to serve people. They prefer facts to hunches. They are called *organized* people, because they take the logical approach to things. Sometimes Thinkabout Owls prefer gray or other light, soft, natural colors, as well as earth tones.

The Thinkabout Owl is the Earth Keeper

Thinkabouts take things in as information, rules, data, past experiences. Thinkabouts are comfortable asking questions, listening, and watching others. Thinkabouts prefer to gather information and think about it in careful, factual ways. They find patterns in nature and things to help them create order. That's why Thinkabouts are neat people who put everything back in the right place. Thinkabouts need time to think things over and make decisions. They work to keep the world a safe place where things will stay the same because they see the natural patterns  in life. They always see the risks of change; thats why their glass is half empty. They ask, "What's missing in this idea?" They like things done the right way. They do have feelings and fears, though they rarely put them into words. They are stressed when there is no order or stability. They can become negative, unfriendly, and stubborn in order to get things to go in their particular "right and narrow way."

The Lookabout Lion Leads Tomorrow

Lookabout Lions are left-brained. They love knowledge. They prefer to think more than feel. They are called *visual* people because they prefer to look about their surroundings and picture things in their minds. Lookabout Lions prefer bold, vivid primary colors.

The Lookabout Lion Sees Vision-Logic

Lookabouts activate things — plans, leadership, authority and results. Lookabouts are comfortable answering questions, talking, and expressing themselves. Lookabouts see how everything could be made better. They like to do things their own way. They can envision a plan and explain it very convincingly. They take control of the best ideas and facts and get results. Lookabouts own the glass. They like to get to the point; they are willing to take risks and make decisions quickly. Lookabouts are both neat and messy people. They keep a lot of things stuffed  in their drawers. They take charge, involve others, and get results. Lack of choice, independence, or vision may cause Lookabouts stress. They can be hostile and bossy, yelling to get their own way... others get the highway.

The Feelabout Koala Tugs Hearts

Feelabout Koalas are right-brained and love action. They prefer to feel more than think. They are called *kinesthetic* people, which means they are sensitive to how their emotions and bodies feel. They prefer warm, soft, quiet, pastel colors. Feelabout Koalas take the journey of the heart inside out.

The Feelabout Koala is the Peace Maker

Feelabouts understand such things as feelings=emotions, movement, and impressions. They are friendly people, good at coordinating gatherings because they are cheerful and like to bond, doing things in harmony. Feelabouts are adaptive and flexible; they don't like to disagree because they feel caught in the middle of both sides. To them the glass is both half-full and half-empty. They want to know the concerns of the group, and to be helpful, a part of things. Feelabouts are clever at making things by hand and learn by doing. They like to make things up as they go. Feelabouts are both messy and neat people who save up a lot of memorabilia. They may hold anger and worries inside rather than speak up and risk a quarrel. Lack of *harmony* or a sense of not belonging may cause them stress. They can be whiny, gossipy, thin-skinned, or sneaky in order to get their own way. Being left out or alone is the worst for these nurturers.

Relating to Others

On the next page, pretend you are looking down at the top of a family tree, stretching from its four live clusters.

It's growing from four root values — just like we do — and the rings of life compressed within its trunk (the heart of your spirit core).

Find your strongest root value and write your name among the leaves growing there. Next, think about the people you live with — your family, friends, etc.

Put each one's name among the group of leaves growing from the root value you think is the most real and true for them —

order, freedom, understanding, harmony.

Next, draw branches connecting your name to each of the other names. Draw thick strong branches to the people you feel close to — those who listen to and understand you the most.

Draw thinner, weaker branches to those who don't relate to you very well. Draw broken branches toward those with whom you have trouble.

Growing Parts of You

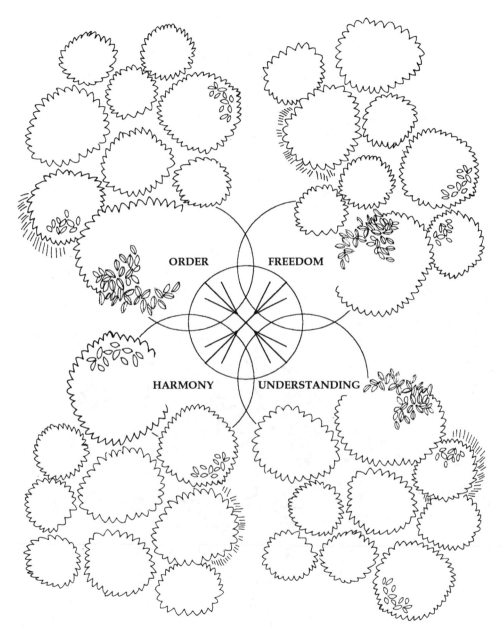

ORDER   FREEDOM

HARMONY   UNDERSTANDING

Family is Our Growing Edge

Thinkabout Owl   **Lookabout Lion**

Feelabout Koala   **Talkabout Chimp**

Alex's Sample

Uu is for us   Alex 1970
                      Xx is for eXtra love
                      dad   mom

                      parent Alex
           liza

Alex loves bonding and family reunions

Root values such as caring and commitment to family begin early in our development. When these values are nurtured and supported, we develop caring relationships throughout our lives.

Color and Connect Your Family Profile

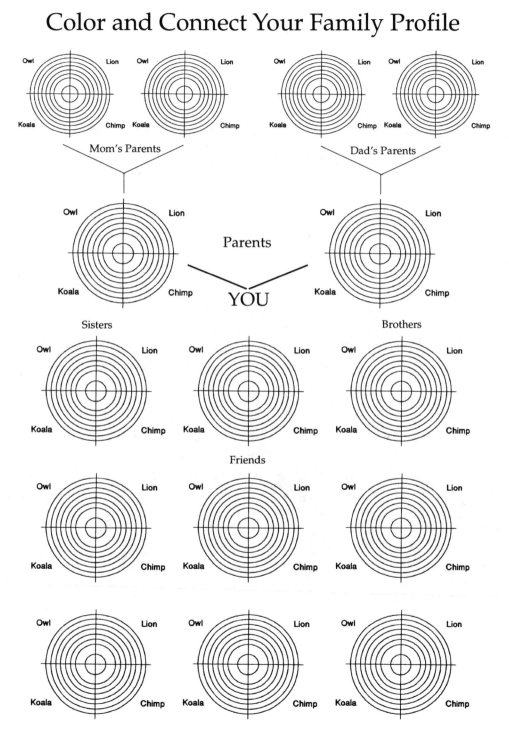

*"A poem in a child there always is to be.
A poem in a child is always to go free."*
Liza Reverman (eight years old)

Your Thoughtfulness is a Work of Heart

Lookabout Lion, Talkabout Chimp, Feelabout Koala, and Thinkabout Owl all name their troubles and tell themselves, "Now I'll learn from the rest and be my best when I am part of the whole." Thinkabout Owl, Lookabout Lion, Talkabout Chimp, and Feelabout Koala learn how to stay healthy and have fun through all of the work and the play, one and all, every day. Each is a part of the whole.

If your heart could talk you would hear a larger self, the Thinkabout, Lookabout, Talkabout, Feelabout parts in yourself — the parts close to your heart. Have you ever wondered why some groups of people work well together and others don't? Some have "Synergy Sense," when all four of your senses work together to solve problems. Synergy Pals are always more than the sum of their parts.

161

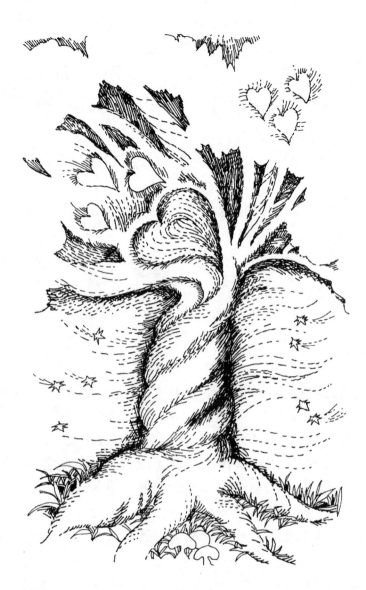

"Wisdom is the tree of Life to those who embrace her; those who lay hold of her will be blessed."
Proverbs 3.18 NIV

Glossary
Resource Words for Adults

Adaptive—One's ability to adjust to circumstances; how the Synergy Pals work collaboratively as a team to find methods to tackle problems.

Affiliate—The need people have to associate with one another. In synergistic terms, learning to work harmoniously as a team, balancing tolerances and biases.

Anchor—A stimulus arising from experience that, when applied, elicits a specific response: pain or pleasure.

Anxiety—Vague apprehension or fear about the future.

Auditory—Using one's ears as the primary way to perceive the world and access information.

Away From—A tendency to move in a reverse direction, away from someone or something perceived as bringing pain.

Belief—A general expectation or assumption about the way the world operates or other people behave. Beliefs are based on one's experience, temperament and values are learned and can be unlearned or changed.

Chimp, Talk-about—Auditory needs lots of "room" for ideas and creativity; who needs to share and discuss with others, whose opinions they value; and who needs to feel understood on a deep level. Enjoys shaking things up a bit, possibly out of boredom or for shock value. Enthusiast needs follow-through pals. See **Explorer/Planner**.

Common Ground—When two or more people feel a connection on some level personally, they share a bond, value, belief, experience, need, personality trait, or feeling about a certain situation.

Communication—Exchanging information using verbal or written language and/or various behavioral signals.

Content—The subject matter of life events and/or interactions with others, around which **process** happens.

Decision—Judgment to move away from pain and towards pleasure.

Detailer—A person with a natural talent for noticing, appreciating, planning for, and executing small but often extremely important details. Perfectionist , given high standards, finishes what is started.

Digital—Using language as the primary way to perceive the world and access information.

Disassociation—Retaining a memory without being connected to the feelings associated with the remembered experience.

Dream Mover—Someone who talks about fun and inspired ways to do things. See **Chimp, Talk-about** and **Explorer/Planner**.

Ecology—The study of how the individual affects the whole, the whole affects the individual, and the total relationship between an individual and his or her external environment. Internal ecology is concerned with the relationships among one's own values, beliefs, expectations, and behavior as one moves toward his or her unlimited potential.

Explorer—A person whose natural talents enable him or her to think out and consider new and different ways of accomplishing things.

Extrovert—One whose behavior is oriented more in an outward direction, toward other people and external circumstances.

Freedom (Rhythms)—The space and lack of restrictions to make choices, conventional or innovative; to think up and explore new and diverse ideas; and to be boldly creative, without offending others. Also, the space and opportunity to express oneself.

Gestalt—The whole picture; the breadth and depth of whatever surrounds one's (usually narrower) focus. When one can see the "whole," the "detail" can be kept in perspective.

Harmony (Rhythms)—The peaceful coexistence of everyone concerned. It is not necessary for everybody to agree on every little thing for harmony to exist; however, it is absolutely necessary for each person to respect the opinions, feelings, ideas, needs, space, and values of everyone else involved.

Inertia—A tendency to remain in a given state, one's comfort zone, resulting in lack of challenge and growth.

Introvert—One whose behavior is oriented more in an inward direction, toward internal conditions.

Kinesthetic—Using one's emotional or tactile senses as the primary ways to perceive the world and access information.

Koala, Feel-about—Kinesthetic needs emotional harmony, connection, empathy, touching (hugs), and personal contact with friends and loved ones. Feel-about Koala needs to have a secure sense of belonging. Retreats to avoid conflict. His or her own feelings and those of others, are major motivators. See **Nurturer**.

Language—There are two levels of language: one's accustomed verbal means of communication (speaking and hearing words), and different individual "thinking languages"— internal/mental communication, which may be visual, auditory, kinesthetic, or analytical.

Learning Style—An individual's preferred means of acquiring and remembering new information (see **Auditory**, **Digital**, **Kinesthetic**, and **Visual**).

Lion, Look-about—Visual-A big-picture person who needs options and choices, as well as challenges, and is driven to get results; a visionary, and free spirit. See **Planner/Explorer**.

Map—See **Paradigm**.

Matcher/Matching—Comparing input with known information to determine if it is harmonious or not.

Metaphor—A story that conveys a deeper meaning, symbolizing how something works or what it means. The "Synergy Tree" story is a metaphor.

Opposites---attract so we can learn to develop our weaknesses as well as our strengths. The more we learn to interact opoosites discover how to create synergy from the inside out. Opposites are more than the sum of their parts.

Order (Rhythms)—The sense of calm that may result from having a place for everything and everything in its place. Having a schedule, or rhythm to one's day or a particular project.

Owl, Think-about—Digital-A person who looks at the facts of a project or situation; who needs to feel safe and is most comfortable when things are done in an orderly fashion, in an environment where everything is in its place. One who notices, as well as provides, details. See **Detailer**.

Nurturer—A person with a natural talent for soothing and encouraging others.

Paradigm—A map, framework, or pattern on which to base a belief system. For example, the world was once thought to be flat and then known to be round: the change in thinking about the shape of the world was a "paradigm shift".

Part—A portion of one's personality — the "parts" of Think-about Owl, Talk-about Chimp, Feel-about Koala, and Look-about Lion "parts" within each individual.

Peace Maker—Someone who negotiates an easier way for people to do things. See **Koala, Feel-about** and **Nurturer**.

Peer Socialization----is at the heart of social acceptance. Why children turn out the way they do. Parents matter less than you think and peers matter more with their values, temperament and language as central agents in the story of your making.

Planner—A person whose natural talents allow him or her to be prepared for opportunities that may develop in a given situation; he or she deals with them efficiently, rather then being surprised and/or totally defeated.

Process—The growing, changing, evolving steps that develop around the **content** of events and interactions with others.

Rapport—The sense of trust and harmony felt between people.

Rebellion— A form of adolescent behavior designed to purge the mind of its continuing dependence on mother and father. It is characterized by acts intended to anger and disappoint the parents.

Relativistic thinking—The ability to conceptualize issues from diverse perspectives, various points of view, or different frames of reference. Its emergence signals the onset of youth.

Representational Systems—The five senses [sight, sound (hearing and words), smell, touch, taste] used to convey information to the brain.

Self Actualizing—The act of developing a psychological ability within one's own mind—first through understanding a newly emerging ability and then through granting oneself permission to develop the ability. Achieving the capacity to self-actualize enables one to become self-developing and obviates the need for actualizers.

Skill Master—Someone who considers the correct way to do things and likes follow-through. See **Owl, Think-about** and **Detailer.**

State—The status and sum total of what one thinks, feels, and does at any given time. How emotions are managed may depend upon the given circumstances. Resolution propels us towards co-operation.

Synergy—The result of interactions of heterogeneous parts multipying the effect of the whole. The whole equals more than the sum of the parts. The interrelatedness of life; people are unique, yet more alike than different, and we are all creatively connected in some way.

Temperament—One's natural behavior or method of action, based on personality. A Synergy Pal, for example, may behave primarily as a Think-about Owl but also have Talk-about Chimp, Look-about Lion, and Feel-about Koala aspects to his or her personality and behavior; order, understanding, freedom, harmony are anthropomorphic values or metaphors for consistently driven behaviors.

Toward—A preference to move closer to pleasure associated with someone or something.

Unconscious functioning—occurs outside of psychological awareness.

Understanding (Rhythms)—The ability to not only listen to someone, but to also comprehend what is being said. Empathizing rather than just sympathizing with a loved one's pain (given that friends are loved ones); the capacity to feel, not just observe.

Value—One's individual (or a group's) priorities, against which people and events are measured for worthiness; for instance, Order, Freedom, Understanding, and Harmony are values, that, if denied, cause suffering.

Vision Leader—Someone who seeks for a new way to do things. See **Lion, Look-about** and **Explorer/Planner.**

Visual—Using one's eyes as the primary way to perceive, access information.

Youth—the stage of life that follows adolescence and is characterized by the ability to think relativistically.

Recommended Reading

Alessandra, Anthony, & M.J. O'Connor, *The Platinum Rule,* Warner Books, 1996.

Anderson, Clifford, M.D., *The Stages of Life,* Atlantic Monthly Press, 1995.

Bandler, Grinder, & Satir,Virginia, *Changing With Families,* S&B. Books, 1976.

Berrien, Polly, *Whole Child/Whole Parent,* Harper & Row, 1983.

Buzan, Tony, *Brain $ell,* McGraw Hill, 1997.

Briggen, Peter R., M.D., *Reclaiming Our Children,* Perseus Books, 2000.

Buckingham, Marcus & Coffman, Curt, *First Break All The Rules,* SimonSchuster, 1997.

Campbell, Joseph, *The Hero With A Thousand Faces,* Pantheon, 1949.

Canfield, Jack & Hansen, Mark Victor *Chicken Soup-Mega Series,* HC. Inc., 1993.

Carey, William, M.D., *Understanding Your Child's Temperament,* MCM Press, 1997.

Chopra, Deepak, M.D., *Perfect Health,* Harmony Books, 1990.

Coleman, Daniel, *Emotional Intelligence,* Bantam Books, 1995.

Coles, Robert, *The Moral Intelligence of Children,* Random House, 1997.

Copland, Dunn, and Treffing, *Bringing Out Giftedness in Your Child,* Wiley, 1992.

Covey, Stephen, *The Seven Habits of Highly Effective Families,* Golden Books, 1997.

Dawkins, Richard, *Unweaving the Rainbow,* Houghton Mifflin, 1998.

D'Adamo, Peter J., M.D., *Eat Right 4 Your Type,* G.P. Putnam's, 1996

De Bono, Edward, *De Bono's Thinking Course,* Facts on File Publications, 1985.

Dent, Jr., Harry, *The Roaring 2000s,* Simon & Shuster, 1998.

Domingez Joe & Vicki Robin, *Your Money or Your Life,* Viking Penguin, 1992.

Erickson, Milton, *My Voice Will Go With You,* Norton Co. Inc., 1982.

Friedman Thomas, *The Lexus and The Olive Tree,* Simon & Schuster, 1999.

Gallagher, Winfred, *I.D.,* Random House, 1996.

Gardner, Howard, Ph.D., *Leading Minds: Anatomy Leadership,* BasicBooks, 1995.

Gelb, Michael J., *How to Think Like Leonardo DaVinci,* Delacorte Press, 1998.

Gladwell, Malcolm, *The Tipping Point,* Little, Brown and Company, 2000.

Gottman, John, *The Heart of Parenting,* Simon & Schuster, 1997.

Gurian, Michael, *The Wonder of Boys,* G.P. Putnam, 1996.

Hammer, D., *Living with Our Genes,* Doubleday Press, 1998.

Harris, Judith, *The Nature Assumption,* The Free Press, 1998.

Herrmann, Ned, *The Creative Brain,* Brain Books, 1990.

Hillman, James, *The Soul's Code,* Random House, 1996.

Hoff, Benjamin, *The Tao of Pooh,* E.P. Dutton, 1982.

Jacobs, Robert W., *Real Time Strategic Change,* Berrett-Koehler Pub. Inc., 1994.

Johnson Robert, *Balancing Heaven and Earth,* HarperCollins, 1998.

Jung, Carl, *Man and His Symbols,* Doubleday, 1964.

Keirsey D. and Bates, M., *Please Understand Me,* Prometheus Nemesis, 1978.

Littauer, Florence, *Personality Plus,* Fleming H. Revell, 1998.

Marshall,I.&Zohar D., *Who's Afraid of Schodingers Cat?,* Morrow&Co., 1997.

Myers, Isabel Briggs and Peter, *Gifts Differing,* Consulting Psy Press, 1980.

Perkins David, *Outsmartig IQ,* Simon & Schuster, 1995.

Pipher, Mary, Ph.D., *Rebuilding Our Families,* Ballantine Books, 1996.

Rico, Gabrielle, *Writing the Natural Way,* J.P. Tarcher, 1983.

Robbins, Anthony, *Unlimited Power,* Fawcett Columbine, 1986.

Russell, Peter, *The Global Brain,* J.P. Tarcher, 1983.

Shick, Lyndall, M.A., *Understanding Temperament,* Parenting Press, 1998.

Smith, Lendon, M.D., *Improving Your Child's Behavior Chemistry,* S&S, 1989.

Stanislaw Joseph & Yergin Daniel, *Commanding Heights,* S&S, 1998.

Sternberg, Robert J., Ph.D., *The Nature of Creativity,* Cambridge, 1988.

Sternberg, Robert J., Ph.D., *The Nature of Creativity,* Cambridge, 1988.

Stevens, Laura J., *12 Effective Ways to Help Your ADD/ADHD Child,* 2000.

Tannen, Deborah, Ph.D., *The Argument Culture,* Random House, 1999.

Tracy, Brian, Ph.D., *Maximum Achievement,* Simon & Schuster, 1996.

Tobias, Cynthia U., *Every Child Can Succeed,* Focus on the Family, 1996.

Waldrop, M.M., Ph.D., *Complexity: Edge of Order&Chaos* Add Wes, 1996,

Wilbur Ken, *A Brief History of Everything,* Shambala, 1996.

Wilson, Edward, O. Ph.D., *Consilience,* Random House, 1998.

Zemke, Raines & Filipczak, *Generations At Work,*
     Amacom, 2000.

"I keep six honest serving men
(they taught me all I knew);
Their names are What and Why and When;
And How and Where and Who."
Rudyard Kipling

Acknowledgments
My Own Family Tree

Every tree needs good soil for deep taproots, so it can receive the nourishment that gives it the supple strength to bend and grow. The soil from which this book grew is deep and rich: the insights of many who have studied the complexities of the new brain/mind research have greatly helped to nourish my work.

Many people gave me the gift of their time, talking to me and contributing their expertise to this work. My colleagues in the American Creativity Association, and the National Speakers Association continually remind me that mutual respect is the foundation for expanding everyone's creativity. It has been the work of the brave brain, by the curious and courageous of every culture. Their mysteries began in ancient times, with the search for the god within, and continue with the work of scientists and natural philosophers. Each discovery suggests that another possibility exists, creating new discoveries. During the past century discovery has been truly amazing. Reconciliation propels us.

The human brain is designed to read meanings into things even when the things have no meaning except the meaning we give it.

My own roots, as well as the roots of this book, come from a mixture of frustration, patience, and curiosity. All is grounded in my strong belief that all problems have solutions, a belief I inherited from my first role models. My mother, Ella Hellmann Urbigkeit, an immigrant full of hope and determination, followed her interests against all odds and became a builder. My father, Edward Charles Urbigkeit, expressed his emotional nature through music and by empathizing with others. Their values sprung from different ways of approaching life and their early cultural conditioning. Because they didn't speak each other's emotional language, it was sometimes difficult for them to understand each other. Though they loved and respected one another and found a way to work together intuitively, their struggle to understand and relate to each other was not easy for them or for their children. They had no information about temperament types or emotional needs. The society they lived in was more rigid about religion, culture and gender expectations. The intuitive support of my brothers, Eldon, Oliver, and Stanley, was invaluable to me then, as it is now. I continue to love and learn from them.

The roots of my life and work grew into a strong trunk of emotional support from longtime friends and colleagues who, in living, have provided material for this book. Heartfelt thanks to Emelia Rathbun, who defined the wise concept of right relationship (living your own life on purpose and with passion), and to Eva Marie Vasiljevic, my spiritual mother, who has always given me her unconditional love. Her wisdom tells us: Love survives when wisdom has an effective voice. Knowing what to do with information is real wisdom.

As this book grew, my learning branched out in new and diverse directions. I am especially grateful to illustrator Charlotte Lewis, who made my dream pictures come true, thanks to her different and impressive visual language in a different language of the brain. Seoni Baird gave her thoughtful consideration to the organizing and shaping of a vast body of raw information, bringing it into a coherent whole. Many others edited, laid out text and tailored designs to my specifications. Carol Qutub generously provided a room with an ocean view so I could work. Richard Ferguson of Maxim Graphics helped with cover design. Confidently Gardner Mein, Karen Muthreich, Bob Smith and Joan Pinkert, fine-tuned the end product. Thank you all, your consideration is a work of heart.

My personal growing edge, which is always stretching toward new experiences, is nurtured by the encouragement as well as the struggle of my family. I thank my children, Peter, Alex, and Liza, and my husband Jack, who first unfolded the mystery of human creativity for me. Together all of us continue to grow, with endless curiosity, toward the purpose of this book searching for a family soul.

My family helped me grasp the significance of shared experience, how necessary deeply rooted connections are for a family to love and learn from one another. And now Kristin Swaner Reverman, Kerry Cress Reverman and Gabriel Dansky are showing me anew the bonds of kinship. Love attracts new life, forming bodies of ever greater complexity: Our granddaughters, Caroline Wells and Eloise Cathryn, serve as beautiful reminders that the miracle of life starts inside another human being; this is how truly we are made to interact with each other.

Like the miracle of life, love renews itself over and over again. Experience is a mystery of failure and repair. Resolution propels us in the struggle to be alive and evolve. The notion of consciousness to the universe has been transformed in this century by the amazing picture of earthrise. Showing us beings to becoming in our longing for joyful exchange. An ecology of souls reflects the ecology of nature; nature needs everyone's genius to improve this planet a little more for our grandchildren, the timeless faces yet to be conceived.

To my family, I express my love and appreciation. Family reveals the secrets of personalities — the laughing and crying together over shared mistakes and successes. Experiences bring some failures and repairs. Every crisis presents a choice: be safe or be brave and change. Together we are on an adventure of forgiveness as we learn how to best love one another. I draw from these soils — souls — of inspiration and these springs of love as they continue to bring me into being. This is how my book grew: this is how we learn about flowers from petal to root. May we all find the courage to keep growing and blooming, again and again.

love of daughter
Vrely

171

Index

"If you have to eat a frog, do it first thing in the morning."
Mark Twain

New Learning Model for School Instruction Critical to Student's Survival.

There exists a devastating 50% non-completion rate amongst kids in USA high schools, and it is not for a lack of quality teachers or concerned parents. So WHAT exactly is the problem?

Why are our kids not succeeding in schools? And what can be done about it? Societal shifts from decade to decade have never occurred so rapidly or on such a global scale as in this new millennium. Our children are growing up in a society of instant gratification, weekly mergers and corporate takeovers, drive-thru fast food, on-line shopping and programmable TV designed to suit the desires of the individual. Add to this the readily available distractions of sex, drugs, body mutilation and other forms of seductive self-destruction, and our kids are on the fast track to troubled nowhere. Furthermore, this frightening world causes parents to sometimes forego discipline in favor of over-protectiveness as a matter of preservation.

Traditional "linear" models of teaching no longer serve the needs of today's school students. How many of us have heard our student ask"But, how will learning to calculate the area of an irregular polygon help me to become a successful dance instructor/dot.com executive / pro-baseball player?

Teachers, school administrators and parents need to learn a new brain-based model that will catch those failing students in the net of success. This new model of learning integrates all areas of the brain into a synergistic whole, and will make the lives of teachers and parents much easier. Parents will have a healing plan to reclaim their children. Teachers will escape the frustration they currently experience in their chosen field and will find renewed energy when they see the effects of this new model on their students'comprehension and retention of material.

You can learn more at www.synergypals.com or call 1 800 241 PALS(7257) or write via e-mail to drardy4u@aol.com

173

Products and Services

To order additional copies or receive quantity discount information

www.synergypals.com or Phone Order Line or 1-800-241-PALS (7257)

FAX Order Line (503) 245-6759 E-Mail- drardy4u@aol.com- www.synergypals.com

Book-Series 1 : *Team-Smart* SQ

BOOKS	CASES	PRICE/DISCOUNT
1-23	(24 bks)	$14.95 each book
24-96	1–4	10% discount
120–266	5–11	30% discount
288	12	40% discount

Outside USA: add 10% of Total Price.

❑ Shipping&Handling add % 10% in the US

Add 15% foreign orders _____ Total (US $)

❑ NO RETURNS

❑ Prices may change without notice.

❑ Simply supply us a name and address to forward books as gifts.

❑ RUSH DELIVERY: I cannot wait 3 weeks for book rate. Here is $6.95 for Priority Mail.

Sense-sational Synergy Pals Series

PACKAGE	PKGS	PRICE/DISCOUNT
1-23	(24 packages)	$89.95 each Package
24-96	1–4	10% discount
120–266	5–11	30% discount
288	12	40% discount

BUY SERIES For $195.00 AND SAVE $35.00

1. *Team-Smart-*SQ. – book @ $14.95
2. *Teamwork is Child's Play* – book @ $14.95
3. *The Heartmaster* – book @ $14.95
4. *Four Kinds of Smart* – poster & song tape @ $25.00
5. *Synergy Pals* – card deck @ $10.00
6. *Who Wants To Be A Synergy Pal?* – board game @ $25.00
7. *The Heart Master* – story apron & audio tape @ $45.00
8. *GreasyGrimyGopherGuts* – tape & song book @ $25.00
9. Certified presenter of core programs kit @ $50.00

www.synergypals.com, fax, call, e-mail, ORDERS

TOTAL AMOUNT DUE: _____ for _____ BOOKS and/or _____ PKG

COMPANY NAME: _____

NAME: _____

ADDRESS: _____

CITY: _____ STATE: _____ ZIP: _____

VISA OR M.C.# _____ EXP. DATE: _____

Bill my: ❑ MasterCard ❑ Visa   I have enclosed: ❑ check ❑ money order

SIGNATURE _____

We accept Master Card and VISA or send check or money order to:

Synergy Pals Int'l
3058 SW Fairmount Blvd
Portland, Oregon 97201-1439

In House Training Seminars for Corporations and Associations

Dr. Ardy will keynote your business or participating organizations.
Group, training, consulting, lecture, rates available. *Call 800- 241 PALS*